Spoon Carving
PROJECT BOOK

Emmet Van Driesche

Fox Chapel
PUBLISHING

Photo Credits: Ben Gancsos

Managing Editor: Gretchen Bacon
Acquisitions Editor: Kaylee J. Schofield
Editor: Joseph Borden
Designer: Chris Morrison
Indexer: Jay Kreider

ISBN: 978-1-4971-0297-2

LCCN: 2022946152

To learn more about the other great books from Fox Chapel Publishing, or to find a retailer near you, call toll-free 800-457-9112 or visit us at *www.FoxChapelPublishing.com*.

We are always looking for talented authors. To submit an idea, please send a brief inquiry to acquisitions@foxchapelpublishing.com.

Printed in China
First printing

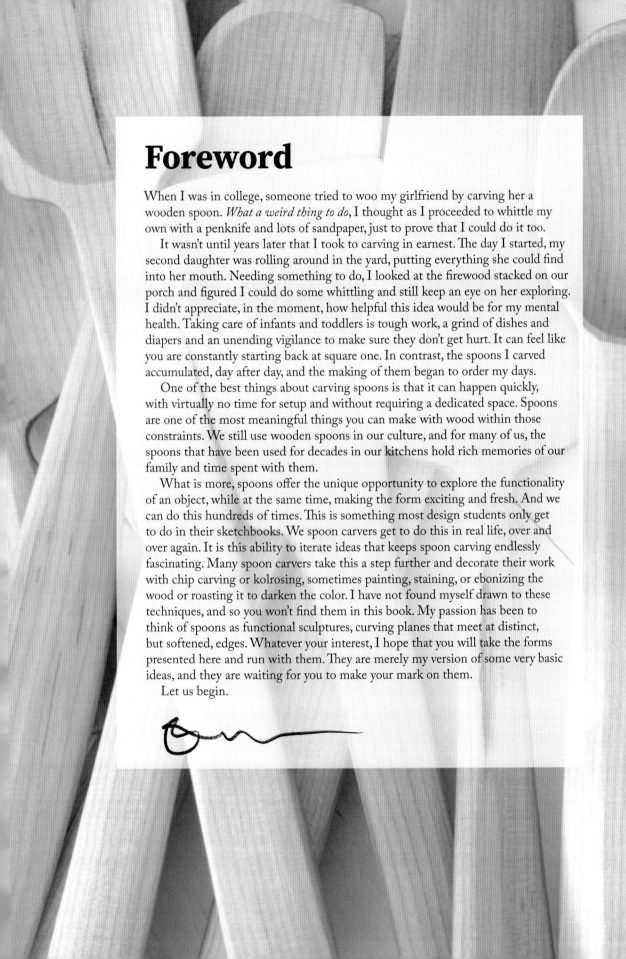

Foreword

When I was in college, someone tried to woo my girlfriend by carving her a wooden spoon. *What a weird thing to do*, I thought as I proceeded to whittle my own with a penknife and lots of sandpaper, just to prove that I could do it too.

It wasn't until years later that I took to carving in earnest. The day I started, my second daughter was rolling around in the yard, putting everything she could find into her mouth. Needing something to do, I looked at the firewood stacked on our porch and figured I could do some whittling and still keep an eye on her exploring. I didn't appreciate, in the moment, how helpful this idea would be for my mental health. Taking care of infants and toddlers is tough work, a grind of dishes and diapers and an unending vigilance to make sure they don't get hurt. It can feel like you are constantly starting back at square one. In contrast, the spoons I carved accumulated, day after day, and the making of them began to order my days.

One of the best things about carving spoons is that it can happen quickly, with virtually no time for setup and without requiring a dedicated space. Spoons are one of the most meaningful things you can make with wood within those constraints. We still use wooden spoons in our culture, and for many of us, the spoons that have been used for decades in our kitchens hold rich memories of our family and time spent with them.

What is more, spoons offer the unique opportunity to explore the functionality of an object, while at the same time, making the form exciting and fresh. And we can do this hundreds of times. This is something most design students only get to do in their sketchbooks. We spoon carvers get to do this in real life, over and over again. It is this ability to iterate ideas that keeps spoon carving endlessly fascinating. Many spoon carvers take this a step further and decorate their work with chip carving or kolrosing, sometimes painting, staining, or ebonizing the wood or roasting it to darken the color. I have not found myself drawn to these techniques, and so you won't find them in this book. My passion has been to think of spoons as functional sculptures, curving planes that meet at distinct, but softened, edges. Whatever your interest, I hope that you will take the forms presented here and run with them. They are merely my version of some very basic ideas, and they are waiting for you to make your mark on them.

Let us begin.

Table of Contents

38

106

52

84

90

96

114

70

Getting Started

There are many ways to carve a spoon, but all the projects in this book follow a similar pattern. A fresh bit of wood is broken down from a tree trunk or limb, and then an axe and hand saw are used to shape that chunk into something resembling the desired form. At that point, some combination of straight and hook knives is used to shape the wood to its final form, and then it is burnished and treated before use. When viewing photos of me shaping the wood, please keep in mind that I am left-handed, and you should adjust your grip according to what suits you best following the guidelines I have laid out.

There's nothing sacred about doing it this way. You could cut your spoons out of milled lumber using a band saw, use a rasp and gouge to shape them, and then sand them to a final surface. But you would have a hard time recreating many of the details of the forms, and much of the point of this book would be lost. More than a compendium of forms, this book is an extended lesson in how to carve spoons in this way. Each project builds on the one before it, adding the next layer of complexity, and so to walk through the forms of this book is to establish a vocabulary of much of what is possible in this style of carving. Fluency, of course, comes with repetition and deliberate practice, but attempting each of these forms, in order, is an excellent start.

Key Terms

- **Bevel.** A beveled edge is an edge that is not perpendicular to the face(s) of the piece being worked. It is used to soften the edge of a piece. There is some overlap between this term and chamfer.

- **Billet.** The billet is the piece of wood that is left over once you have chopped your log or branch down to size. This is the first thing you will need to create before beginning any of these projects.

- **Crank/crank face.** A crank or crank face is a very shallow V that establishes the line of a handle and the line of the top of the bowl of a spoon or blade.

- **Camber.** A camber is a slight convexity, arching, or curvature. To camber a piece is to create a curve upward in the middle.

- **Chamfer.** To chamfer a piece is to knock off the corners at the edge of a facet. This can be done precisely, but loosely works just as well.

- **Facet.** To facet a piece is to create multiple sides by carving or axing them into the wood's surface. A facet is one of these sides.

- **Microchamfer.** A very small chamfer.

- **Taper.** To taper a piece is to make it become progressively smaller or narrower toward one end.

Why I Cut My Own Wood

All wood was once a tree. Obvious, right? But many ways of using and working with wood obscure this fact—sometimes by how the material is processed before you encounter it, and sometimes by the tools used to manipulate it. We have gotten good at these things, and it is possible to work with wood in many ways that almost completely ignore how it existed as a tree.

Not so with the projects in this book.

You will be devastatingly aware that the material you are using was once a living organism. More than that, you will be aware of exactly where the material came from, how it relates to the larger tree, and why it will or won't do what you want. You will fail in some of these projects because of the piece of tree you chose. You will succeed in others, largely because you managed to attain some sort of synchrony between what you were trying to achieve and what the wood was willing to do.

Wood is like that. It is your partner in this process, and when you use a knife or axe, it is an extension of your body, feeling what the wood does in response. The more experience you have, the more you will be able to predict how the wood responds to your action, but there are always surprises, because once again, all wood was once a tree. And trees are individuals.

Maybe the tree you are carving grew up along a windy river, and its fibers reflect that swaying back and forth, interlocked in a tight ripple that makes sense for the tree

but spells frustration for you. Maybe the tree you are carving grew slowly in the shade of other trees for much of its life, putting on the bare minimum growth each year to stay alive, and is dense beyond reason. Maybe it grew out in the open, fast and bounding, and the growth rings are wide and strong. These are things you will come to learn and appreciate.

Breaking down a tree or a limb into usable parts is something everyone should experience at least once, even if you usually need to buy spoon blanks because you live in a city or otherwise find sourcing your own wood impractical. Like watching a butcher break down a side of beef into cuts or learning to harvest vegetables, there is value in understanding where your material comes from, even if you don't always go right back to the source yourself. Part of what this process gives you is an appreciation for how the material differs from one part of the tree to another. Furthermore, each tree is unique and will surprise you. I have split open a perfect log only to find it useless for my purposes, and I have found some of the most beautiful carving wood lurking under several inches of rotten sapwood.

Never forget that this is a dance between yourself and a tree. As you gain experience, you will be able to anticipate what the wood is willing to do. Each of these projects exists in that space, in dialogue with the tree it once was.

The end grain of a piece of wood will crack over time with exposure to air. Sawing off several inches will usually get you back to fresh wood.

In addition, each of us has access to different species of wood and different types of logs or branches. If you live in a city, smaller branches tend to get chipped, whereas larger-diameter chunks are often available if you ask. If you live in the country, you might only have access to the branches in your yard, or you might be able to fell an entire tree. In general, my advice is to stockpile the largest-diameter and longest logs you can. Obviously, this will differ for each person and depend on your available space, capacity for moving them and breaking them down into smaller pieces, and what you can get your hands on.

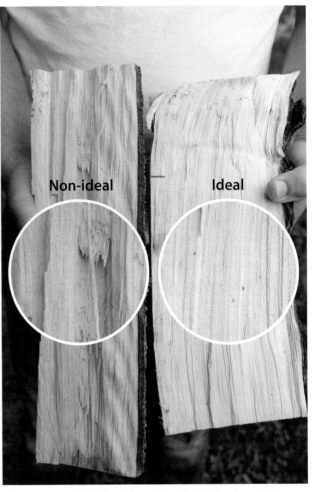

Non-ideal   Ideal

The piece on the left, although technically clear of knots, has too much ripple for spoon carving. Notice how the piece on the right has a more relaxed grain.

Keys to Selecting Wood

- The larger and clearer-grained the piece of wood is, the fewer problems it will give you.
- An exhaustive list of all usable woods would be impossible to include in this book. Birches, maples, walnut, pecan, cherry, fruitwoods (apple, pear, peach, plum), staghorn sumac, avacodo, and poplar are all great carving woods.
- Avoid conifers (pines, spruces, hemlocks, junipers, firs, etc.) or other intensely sapped species like eucalyptus, along with super dense tropical hardwoods that can be toxic.
- Species with lots of tannins (like oaks) or those that are ring porous (oaks and ashes) are worth avoiding unless they are all you can get.
- Look for wood from healthy trees. Rotting or overly dry wood is no good for spoon carving.

So, what do I carve? Well, in my part of the northeast US, the best large-diameter, clear-grained logs I can get my hands on tend to be black cherry and various species of birches and maples. But you might live somewhere with walnut, or tulip poplar, or avocado. So feel it out and you'll be fine.

Please note that I am left-handed, and take that into account as you view the photos of me holding various tools throughout this book.

Introduction to Tools

There is a popularly circulated idea in the spoon carving community that all you need to carve a spoon is three tools: an axe, a straight knife, and a hook knife. This is the equivalent of saying that all you need to cook a meal is a knife and a spatula, ignoring the fact that you need a cutting board, a pan, bowls, utensils, a sink to wash everything in, and a dishrack to dry them. You need more tools than the big three, and the temptation to reduce things to just these is the temptation of the rugged individual, alone in the wilderness. But it's just not true, especially when you zoom out from the moment of carving to look at the process as a whole. In reality, here are the tools you will need:

Pruning saw. I like the Silky Professional F180, which has the right size and shape blade, an aggressive bite that allows you to cut large limbs quickly, and a lock-back feature on the handle that allows the blade to be set at two different angles, which I use all the time. This model is both less expensive and better suited to spoon carving than any other model of saw I have come across.

Axe. I use a Gransfors Bruks large Swedish carving axe, symmetrical grind. This is the axe that I recommend to everyone for a number of technical reasons, but it is expensive (around $250). While you save up your money, the best super cheap option is the Fiskars® hatchet. It comes sharp (which can't be said of the other cheap options) and with the right edge geometry and handle shape. In general, I have come to feel that mid-priced tools are not worth it. Start with the cheapest and save for the best.

Club. To use the axe well, you will need a club. This is something you will have to make for yourself. I prefer a club where the head is the junction of two branches, because the interlocking grain at this point keeps the club from cracking apart under the strain of repeated use. To make one like the above, simply get a large-diameter branch with a fork in it, cut off the excess material to create a large head with plenty of striking surface, and cut out a handle that is thin enough to hold comfortably, yet thick and strong enough to withstand repeated blows.

Straight knife. I use straight (or sloyd) knives and hook knives by Matt White of Temple Mountain Woodcraft. These are knives that I helped design, so they are exactly what I want. They are also expensive, and Matt has either a long waiting time or his books are closed, depending on when you catch him. There are starting to be toolmakers whose work is approaching his in quality, but Matt's are still the best as far as I have been able to determine. There's no shortage of sloyd knives on the market, but when you're starting out carving, I recommend the Mora 106 sloyd knife. Don't be tempted by the shorter 120. It feels more manageable to the untrained eye, but it will actually prevent you from being able to do certain things. Generally speaking, a good sloyd knife will be comfortable in your hand, have a full-tang (meaning the metal runs all the way through the handle) construction, and a thicker blade with an upswept curve to promote smooth slicing. (If you're interested in Matt's knives, find him on Instagram @mattwhite_tmw.)

Hook knife. As noted, I use hooks by Matt White. Hooks are one of the hardest tools to get right, as there are so many underappreciated details that matter tremendously in how well the tool works. Thankfully, the Mora 164 just underwent a massive redesign several years ago, changing it from a useless and dangerous tool into an excellent beginner's hook knife. Knife preferences are as varied as the carvers who wield them, but it's fairly accepted that hook knives with a tight curve are the best for beginners. Make sure to get it left- or right-handed, depending on which hand you intend to hold the knife in. Don't be confused; the edge should be facing your body when you hold it, not away from you like you might imagine it should.

Sharpening tools. Having tested all the different sharpening systems and styles, I have come back around to an extremely simple way of sharpening using a wooden block, a length of dowel, and automotive-grade sandpaper. This works better than any other way I have tried, but you need to get a bunch of details right, and it is outside the purview of this book to lay it all out. On page 21, you can find a short overview of the sharpening and stropping process, as well as a QR code that will direct you to my comprehensive sharpening tutorial. I have several videos on this topic on my Reels channel, and I also describe it in exhaustive detail in my book *Greenwood Spoon Carving*, which can be purchased on my website.

Stropping tools. It will become valuable, once you learn to properly sharpen your tools, to be able to strop them. I use a double-sided long strop that I designed myself and a strop stick, both offered by Tom Scandian in Australia. There are some pitfalls to making your own strops, but the most effective cheap alternative is to strop on bare wood. A block or a wooden dowel will work. You can apply stropping compound or not. It will be about half as effective as the kangaroo leather strops that I use, but still worth doing. I use Lee Valley Tools Veritas honing compound. Your strops should either come with slip cases, or you need to keep them wrapped in cloth or a plastic bag. This protects them from collecting dust and grit, and keeps stropping compound from getting on other surfaces. (If you'd like to purchase these tools from Tom, you can find him on Instagram @spoon_carving_with_tom.)

Pen and pencil. It might seem obvious, but part of my process is drawing spoon shapes onto wood, and not every option works well. I use an ultra-bold ballpoint pen for the initial drawing on the spoon, where I need the extra ink flow to counteract the moisture that the wood can have. If the wood is particularly juicy, I use an old, half-used permanent marker, because a fresh one puts out too much ink and can stain the wood more deeply than you want. I use a regular pencil to re-draw the shape halfway through the carving process.

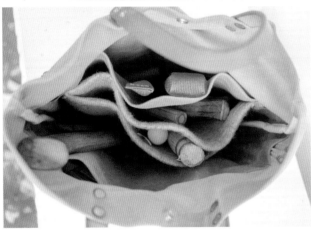

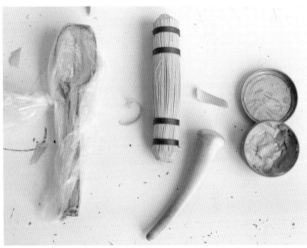

Burnisher. I use a porcelain burnisher and a broomcorn polisher that I designed myself and that I offer for sale. But you can achieve the same effect with a smooth pebble or a bit of antler (which can often be found for sale at a pet store for dogs to chew on), and the side of a broom. These tools are used after carving but before finishing to soften the edges of the work and make work done without sandpaper feel slightly less angular.

Finishing wax. I keep a tin of my finishing wax and a rag on hand so I can finish my work immediately, before the wood has a chance to oxidize or darken. I finish all my work with a homemade 2:1 blend of jojoba oil and beeswax.

Plastic bag. This might seem too trivial to mention, but a plastic bag is actually one of the most important tools in my kit. Every moment I am not actually working on a piece, it is wrapped in the bag to keep it from developing an air-hardened skin.

Toolbox. You will need to keep your tools organized and protected somehow, and be able to carry them around. I use a custom-designed bag made for me by Rural Kind in Wales that allows me to keep everything separated (an important consideration so that dust from sharpening equipment and stropping compound don't get on your tool handles and thus onto your hands, where they will smudge your spoons as you carve), and while you can order one of these from them, they are quite expensive. The best inexpensive solution I have found is the large artist's toolbox from US Art Supply, which can be ordered online. I did have to rip out some internal dividers and replace some flimsy hardware with stuff that was larger and more robust, but I used mine for years and found it to be an excellent fit for keeping everything close at hand and separated. (If you'd like to purchase a bag from Rural Kind, you can find them on Instagram @ruralkind.)

Axe block. An axe block is something you generally need to make yourself. It can be as simple as a stump on the ground that you sit next to in a chair, but there are advantages to having your axe block be high enough that you can stand at it. There are many ways to affix legs to a stump, but the simplest is to tenon in three legs to the underside of the stump. Below, I've included the basic steps to building an axe block. Visit the Learning Resources section on my website (www.emmetvandriesche.com) and download my free book, *The Pocket Book of Axe Blocks*, for a detailed tutorial.

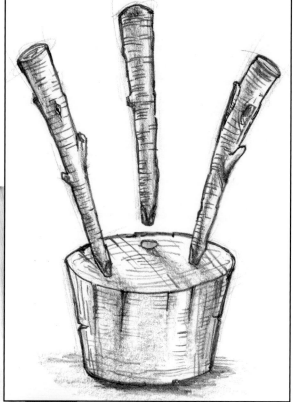

- **Step 1.** Make the legs out of seasoned wood (precut lumber is fine if you don't have anything else lying around that will work), and make them extra long.
- **Step 2.** Trim the legs down to length, cutting each off where it meets the top of your thigh.
- **Step 3.** Drill the holes on the underside of the stump. I use a 1½" (3.8cm) spade bit on a cordless drill to make these, then use the same bit to describe a circle in the end grain of the leg material. This gives me a guide for how much material to remove for the tenons.
- **Step 4.** Pound the legs into the stump good and hard once you've gotten them shaped.
- **Step 5.** Trim the legs as needed and flip the stump right side up.
- **Step 6.** Last, but not least, chop a divot into the top of the axe block so you can press the end of a spoon blank into it and lean it over safely without fear of it slipping.

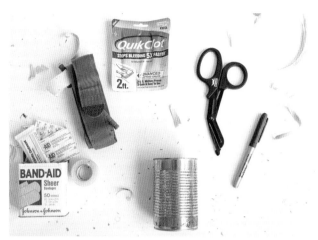

Emergency kit. This is very important and something almost no one talks about because it can seem scary. An axe is a wonderful tool, but as I mentioned earlier, it can be dangerous if you lose focus. Since a bad cut from an axe needs more than just a regular first aid kit, you should have a tourniquet and a hemostatic bandage, also called an Israeli bandage (basically a large bit of gauze impregnated with clay that promotes blood clotting), within arm's reach of your stump in case of emergency. You should have these so they are easily accessible with one hand, and you need to practice putting the tourniquet on your leg just in case. I keep two kits—one indoor and one outdoor. My indoor set is in a drawer in my shop just behind me when I'm at my stump. For my outdoor setup, I keep a second set in a tin can screwed into a stump. You can buy these for a few dollars online, and you absolutely need to get them. I also keep a permanent marker with them to write down the time when I apply the tourniquet (ambitious, I know) and a set of trauma shears, in case I need to cut away any clothing. The trauma sheers are useful because I found, when I did a practice run, that my phone was trapped in my pocket by the tourniquet, and I would need some way to get it out to call for help.

Chainsaw, maul, and wedge. I would be remiss if I didn't mention that I use a chainsaw to process large logs into manageable chunks, and then a splitting maul and wedge to bust open these chunks into pieces that I can then start to split with my carving axe and club. A chainsaw is a dangerous tool, and its use is outside the purview of this book. If you choose to get one, make sure to also buy protective chaps and a helmet, and invest in a safety class. I recently switched to an electric chainsaw, which I have been very pleased with and would recommend to any beginner as the place to start. You will also need a round file and flat file combo tool of the appropriate gauge for sharpening your chain's teeth. I find it helpful to have a vise that I can tap into the top of a stump to clamp the bar in place for convenient sharpening. As for a maul and wedge, I am a fan of the Fiskars® splitting maul and the Estwing Sure Split Wedge; its extra fins are invaluable.

Drill gun and bits. Even if you don't tackle the toast tongs project in this book, a good drill gun is one of the most used tools in our household and well worth getting if you don't already have one. I use a ⅜" (9.5mm) brad point drill bit for the project, and if you want a bit that will help you put legs in an axe block, I use a 1⅜" (3.5cm) spade bit, but 1½" (3.8cm) would be fine, too.

Using the Axe

Nothing in the spoon carving process is quite as dangerous as the axe, both in terms of hurting yourself and also as a major source of repetitive-strain injury if you don't use it properly and pace yourself. Never use the axe when tired or feeling rushed. Stay alert to what you are doing and think through the possible consequences of things not going as planned. All that said, here are the major points to using the axe safely and well:

- **Keep the axe blade several inches away from the hand holding the wood at all times.** There are several ways to do this. The most important is to leave the billet extra long at the start, which gives you room to stay well back from your hand. You can also keep your holding hand safe by pressing down with the heel of your hand with your fingers held out stiffly behind the wood, or by using the tip of your thumb with the fingers tucked up into your palm. Either way, staying away from your hand is the main thing. Keep your motions controlled and small when working near your fingers, and never let the axe come up over your hand.

- **Keep the axe neutral and move the wood underneath it.** Holding the billet straight up and down and moving the axe around as you work on different parts of it seems logical, but it will lead to arm strain and is not nearly as accurate or safe as holding the axe constant and shifting the wood around as needed. Make sure the surface of your axing block has a divot or ledge that you can lodge a corner of the billet into, and keep your axe movement straight up and down.

- **Slow down.** There is a natural tendency to speed up as you get impatient, but fight it. Keep your axing slow and deliberate, and concentrate on the accuracy of your blows. Each one should hit where the previous one left off, allowing you to drive a line down through the wood. If the axe is hitting all over the place, stop and reassess. Chances are you sped up without realizing it, and your arm is fatigued from trying to go too fast (and also possibly from changing the angle of the axe instead of that of the wood).

- **Axing is controlled splitting.** It is using the tendency of wood to split certain ways when force is applied to control the outcome of a situation. For instance, a split tends to run out to the side with less mass instead of simply following the grain. Depending on the line of the spoon and how it interacts with the grain and the overall mass of the billet, sometimes you let this runout occur, and sometimes you deliberately lean into each cut to counteract this force. Sometimes, as when removing wood from the neck, you axe in at an angle that doesn't correspond to the line of the spoon, but that sends a shockwave through the wood that splits it in a way that follows the line. Other times, as on the back of the handle, you chop relief cuts before pushing down to the line you want because it keeps the wood from squeezing the axe.

Using the Sloyd Knife

The sloyd knife is your main tool. It does most of the work when carving and is capable of tremendous power and delicacy. Your ability to control the sloyd knife will, in large part, define your carving experience, yet it is a strange tool to virtually everyone when they begin carving, unlike anything we use in our modern culture. If you treat it the way you would a Swiss Army knife used to point marshmallow sticks, you will damage the tool and hurt yourself or someone around you.

Keeping Safe

There are a few important rules to internalize when it comes to using the sloyd knife. These will minimize the risk of you causing harm, but you will need to be vigilant for a long time before they become muscle memory.

- **Always sheath your knife when it's not in your hand.** This one is simple—the fastest way to damage your blade or end up in the ER getting stitches in your foot is to put your knife down unsheathed. I don't care how brief it is; if you are wiping your nose or going out for a walk, taking a sip of coffee or done for the day, put a sheath on your knife. If it is not in your hand, it should have a sheath on it. End of story.
- **Don't carve when angry, rushed, frustrated, or frazzled.** You need your undivided, calm attention on the sharp tool in your hand. Anything less will come back to bite you.
- **Be aware of where the knife will go if things don't go as expected.** Will it hit your leg? Your chest? What's preventing it from cutting your fingers? What about your child or dog?

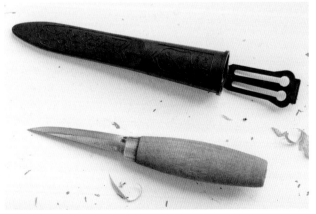

The Cuts

Throughout this book, I will provide more detailed instructions regarding the different cuts as we come to them, so you don't get bogged down here. But there are two main cuts that are worth some explanation right away because they comprise seventy-five percent of everything you will do with the sloyd knife. Understanding how these keep you safe will help you understand why it is important to do them correctly. I will also use this section to touch upon the different cuts you will encounter in the pages ahead.

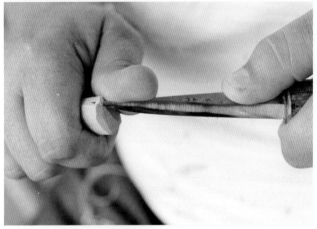

Squeeze cut. Often called a push cut or thumb push cut, I call this the squeeze cut because that more accurately articulates what is going on. When you are doing the sort of cut you would think of as basic whittling, it is easy to mistakenly think that you hold the bit of wood and push the knife through it. In fact, the key is to hold the knife still and pull the wood back against it with the fingers of the hand holding the wood. This is not using your arm, but rather opening and closing the fingers of that hand in a squeezing motion, hence the name. This motion gets transferred accurately to the knife edge by keeping the thumb of your off hand (the hand holding the wood) on the spine of the blade. That thumb-to-spine connection holds the blade in position relative to your off hand, allowing you to move the wood against it. It also forms a pivot point, allowing you to further extend each cut by pulling the handle back and pivoting the blade forward. The rest of the time, the knife hand is controlling the angle the blade presents to the wood but is not generating any power. This is what makes this cut so safe. Not only do you have more power and control this way than if you were trying to shove the knife through the wood, but if the knife exits the wood unexpectedly, there is no forward momentum that will carry it into your leg or someone standing close by.

A squeeze cut is a safer way to move material than what you might think of when you think of traditional whittling. By controlling the amount of pressure and the position of the blade, you can easily remove wood without fear of cutting yourself.

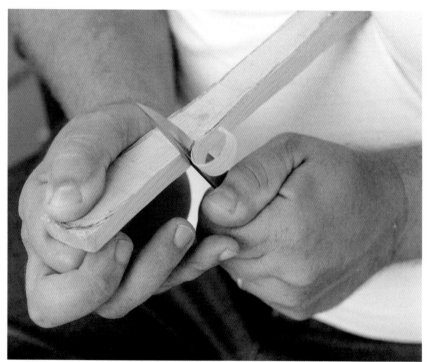

Pull cut. People may tell you that you shouldn't cut toward yourself. This is only true if you don't master how to do the pull cut safely. The first thing to note is that the pull cut always operates with your off hand steadying the wood by pressing it into your sternum and your chest. Never pull toward your hand. The second most important thing is to keep your elbow tight in at your side. As the knife gets closer to you, press more and more of your arm tight until you have the heel of your hand pressed against your chest. This limits the range of motion of the knife to a point where it can't reach you even if it slips out of the wood. The knife should be held straight up and down, with the edge facing toward you and the thumb of your knife hand braced against the side of the blade to stabilize it. And maybe this sounds obvious, but keep your face back from that knife point.

Besides the squeeze cut and pull cut, you will encounter a few other cutting techniques as you go through this book. These will not be utilized as much as the pull cut and squeeze cut. They are:

- **The bump cut.** To perform this cut, place your axe on the mark where you intend to cut, then lift the axe and wood together before bringing them down to split the wood (see page 29).
- **Stop cuts.** A stop cut is made by using a saw to cut into your wood at critical junctures so splitting will not continue past the cut (see page 47).
- **Rim pivot cuts.** There are two of these pivot cuts to learn, one for each side of a spoon's bowl. These cuts employ the use of a stationary pivot point to make a smooth cut along a spoon bowl's rim (see page 75).

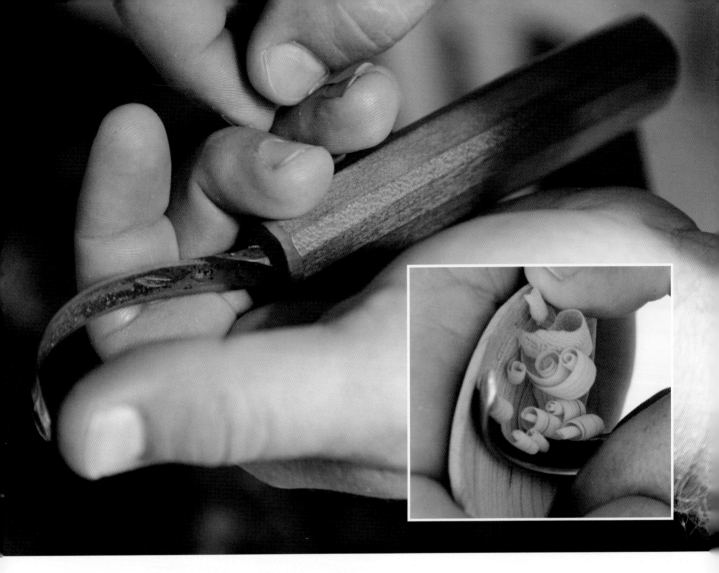

Using the Hook Knife

The hook knife is everyone's nemesis. When you watch someone else use one, it looks so effortless. And then you try it yourself for the first time and you can't even get it to cut. There are two things to using the hook knife well:

1. **Choke up on the blade.** You will need to choke up on the blade much more than you think. The spine of the blade should be against the side of your pointer finger. This gives you more power and greater control; it also eliminates the ability of the knife to cut your thumb, because when you are properly choked up on the blade (even when your fingers are all the way closed), the blade is still ¼" (6.4mm) away from your outstretched thumb. Since you are always pulling toward your thumb, that little distance matters. If you don't choke up on the blade, you *will* cut your thumb.

2. **Using a hook knife is all about understanding grain direction.** There are many cuts you can make: pivoting on the tip of the blade or on the heel, cutting straight across the bowl, or angling across it. But the one cut that won't work, and that is so tempting, is to go from the middle of the bowl up to the tip. It feels like the obvious move, but it's the exact opposite direction of what the grain flow will allow. Instead, think of using the hook knife like you would a shovel. Dig a tiny hole and then slowly enlarge it, going around and around as you go deeper. Start in the middle of the bowl, then work your way out to the edges and down to your desired depth.

Introduction to Sharpening and Stropping

Sharpening is all about getting the edge geometry correct, which for a sloyd knife, is a straight point if you were to look at a cross section of the blade. When dull, the point is blunt, and sharpening gets you down below that blunt point by removing material from either side until you once again have a point. This all happens with the coarsest grit, and if you don't achieve this aim at this stage, no amount of further polishing the edge will help you. I like to start with 400-grit sandpaper wrapped around a wooden block. I like to go towards the knife edge when sharpening, as though I am going to cut the sandpaper, and I alternate passes away from myself with passes towards myself.

Once all secondary bevel is removed, and the cross section is once again a perfect point, I then work my way up through finer sandpaper, roughly doubling the grit until I reach 3,000–5,000 grit. For each jump, I give 12–15 passes on the sandpaper. The goal at this stage is to replace the coarse scratch marks with the next finer ones. But remember, if you haven't eliminated the secondary bevel with the 400 grit, the blade will still be dull.

Stropping is the final stage of sharpening. It can also be done between carving each spoon as a way of keeping your knives sharp longer. As with everything, the details matter.

First, it is best to use a hard leather strop, such as kangaroo or horse butt, that is properly backed by a stiff piece of wood. It is vitally important that the leather is hard and the wood backing it is sufficiently stiff. Any flex in the strop due to squishy leather will end up dulling the edge. The blade pushes down into the leather, which will wrap around the edge. Bare wood with stropping compound on it is preferable if you don't have the proper leather. Apply the compound in a crosshatch pattern and, when it becomes glazed over, scrape it off and reapply. This process applies to wood or leather. Compound should only be applied to the suede side of leather; the strop I use is double-sided, with the smooth leather side acting as the final polish.

Stropping is always done away from the knife edge so there is no danger of cutting the leather, and it is best to use both hands—one on the handle and one pressing down on the tip of the blade to ensure good contact with the strop surface. Five to ten passes per side is fine, but you will get better results with more passes, as long as your form remains clean and you don't roll onto the edge.

For hook knives, a wooden dowel can be used until you have the budget for a kangaroo leather strop stick, and this can be used in the same way as you would use sandpaper wrapped around a dowel to sharpen a hook knife. Strop on the inside of the hook, then use a light touch to strop away any wire burr that has collected on the outside edge. Every strop should have a slip case or a cloth or bag wrapping it, both to keep the strop clean and to keep stropping compound from getting all over your tools.

Key Points

- **Step 1.** Start with 400-grit sandpaper wrapped around a wooden block. Make passes toward the knife edge, as if you're attempting to cut the sandpaper. Alternate with passes toward and away from yourself. Do this until you have removed the secondary bevel and your knife has a sharp point.

- **Step 2.** Repeat this process using progressively higher grits of sandpaper, doubling each grit until you reach 3,000–5,000 grit.

- **Step 3.** Apply a stropping compound in a crosshatch pattern to the suede side of a hard leather that's backed with a stiff piece of wood. If you do not have proper leather, a block of wood is preferable. For hook knives, a wooden dowel or leather-wrapped dowel is required for optimal results.

- **Step 4.** On both sides of the knife, make a minimum of 5–10 passes away from the knife edge. If the leather compound becomes glazed, scrape off and reapply.

Use this code to view my comprehensive sharpening tutorial.

Sourcing Material

Where to Source Material

- Downed limbs in forests or your yard
- Limbs found on the roadside
- Limbs cut from your own land or from someone's who has given you permission
- Purchased online or from a lumberyard (or whever else you might find material that will work)

Chances are good that you started carving because some wood fell into your lap. Someone was pruning a tree, you came across a bit of branch, and you just felt like you had to make something out of it. This is still a fantastic way to get material for spoon carving, particularly if you are in the stage where you are obsessed with carving as many different types of wood as you can. You might even go so far as to carry a folding saw in your backpack or a tarp in your car in case you really score a bonanza. You might find that buying billets from someone is a better use of your time. Everyone is different in how they relate to the craft. For some, finding wood yourself is an integral part of the process. For others, wood is just a material to source, like clay for a potter or fabric for a quilter. Most people with downed limbs in their yard are happy to give you wood if you ask, especially if you explain what you are using it for. Even firewood can be a good source, if it hasn't seasoned too much yet. That's what I started with.

Storing Material

One of the best things you can do to make sure you always have wood to carve is to create a stockpile of material. I'm always sourcing and scrounging material, some from the side of the road, some cut from my own land, and some purchased. I aim to keep the wood in as long a length as I can transport and handle, and I let it age in the log for some time before using it. This can range from several months to more than a year, depending on the species, size, length, and when in the year it was cut.

The main species around me that I must pay attention to the timing of is birch, which will become too spalted (colonized by fungus) over the course of a single summer to remain strong enough to work. So I use that up quickly.

Spalting

Spalting is the colonization of a log by fungus. This can create striking patterns with patches of spalting separated by black lines, which are actually a sort of no-man's-land created when different fungi meet. Spalting is a spectrum, a process that happens over time that you are interrupting at a given point. Depending on how far along the spalting has gotten, the structural integrity of the wood may be compromised. Once the wood is worked and has dried, the spalting will be fixed in time at the point when the moisture content of the wood began to drop. So there is no reason to worry about using and eating off of a spoon made with spalted wood. It is perfectly safe. There are no health concerns with spalted wood that are not inherent to woodworking in general. Sawdust from spalted wood can potentially cause respiratory issues, so if you are processing it with power tools, treat it as you would any other wood and wear proper breathing and eye protection.

Storing your material properly is important to the process no matter how many spoons you intend to carve. If you, like me, have an abundance of wood billets, you will need to find places to store them so the material stays pristine and easily workable.

But most everything else is happy to sit around, mellowing and becoming easier to work. Wood that was squeaky and crunchy when freshly cut becomes waxy and smooth. Many species become significantly easier to carve when aged in the log, and since they lose some moisture content, the resulting spoons are less prone to warping and cracking as they dry, and I can get away with carving from start to finish in one go. When wood is truly fresh, it is so soft that no matter how sharp your knife is, it will tear some fibers instead of cutting them, resulting in a fuzzy surface as the wood dries. Aged wood is dry enough to cut cleanly.

As far as how to store it, I keep mine out of direct sunlight, on a sheet of plywood so it doesn't freeze to the ground, and under cover so I can get to it in the winter. Some people seal the end grain with glue or paint, but I almost never do. The cracks in the end grain that appear as the log dries only extend 1"–2" (2.5–5.1cm) deep, and by keeping the logs as long as possible, I minimize the amount of wood lost to this. If you have the space, you can bust your wood down into billets, bag them up in plastic, and stick them in your freezer. A few minutes of soaking or running under the tap will make the wood ready to work.

Store your billets in the freezer to keep them from cracking.

Food-Safe Finishes

Everyone has their favorite finish. You heat up the oil and watch it sink in. You leave your spoon on a sunny windowsill to cure. You apply lots of thin layers or toss it into a jar of oil to soak up as much as it can. None of these are necessary. The dirty little secret here is that wood needs no finish. It doesn't need to be protected from water or somehow kept elastic and supple. It is just fine on its own—at least for our purposes. There are several reasons I finish my work; the first is to protect it from getting smudged, an important consideration if you are selling your work. The second is to keep the wood from oxidizing and changing its color, although this will still happen, only more slowly. Finally, applying a finish slows down the final drying of the wood, which can help prevent chunkier forms from cracking, as cracks come from the different rates that thin areas and thick areas shrink as they dry out. And, of course, most finishing treatments make the grain pop, which is nice. For optimal results, burnish.

I am not a fan of linseed, tung, or walnut oil. These hardening oils take time to dry, and as they cure, they tend to yellow the wood to a very unattractive color. The first two also taste terrible. Likewise, I am leery of any mixture I would not want to ingest. That includes butcher's wax, cutting board oil, and any number of other products out there. Instead, I use a 2:1 blend of jojoba oil and beeswax. Jojoba oil is hypoallergenic and used in high-end cosmetics. It is easy to work with, tasteless, and neutral in color. This finish is easily mixed up in a tin can in a pot of water on the stovetop. Allow the heat to soften the oil and wax, then combine. Be sure you don't let the water get inside the tin can. I smear it on and wipe it off with a rag. That's it! The piece is immediately ready for use.

Utensil Care

Common wisdom holds that you should only ever wash your wooden utensils by hand and never leave them soaking. I'm not so sure. I leave my spoons soaking in the sink practically every day, and I have experimented with running various ones through the dishwasher, repeatedly. After 25 times through the dishwasher, not only was there no damage, but something about the hot steam of that environment seemed to have brought to the surface some of the innate oils within the wood, restoring its luster in a lasting way. Run that experiment at your own peril, but I think we tend to copy what we see other people saying without testing things for ourselves. When it comes to spoons needing to be refinished, I'm of the philosophy that you just use what's on hand. If that's olive oil, so be it. And never soak your spoons in oil. Nothing good comes of that, as the oil will release over time into your food.

While not strictly necessary, adding a finish to your wood has many benefits.

One option for storing your spoons is making a rack similar to the one pictured here.

Projects

Coat Hook

Approximate length: 5" (12.7cm)

The coat hook is a great place to start if you are new to spoon carving because it gently acquaints you with the tools you will use for other projects, and with the process of collaborating with a tree to make something that combines what you want with what it is willing to give. It is also something you can make with almost no access to wood, since you can harvest appropriate pieces of trees without harming the tree itself. You can find such pieces almost anywhere.

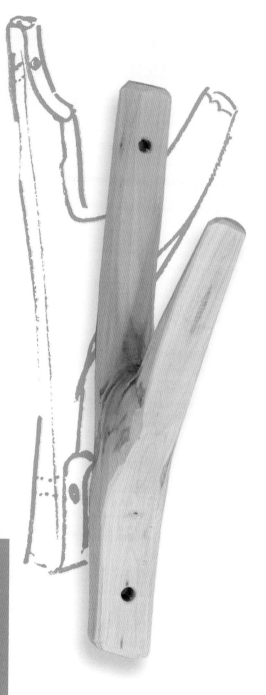

Tools and Materials
- Pruning saw
- Wood
- Axe
- Sloyd knife
- Drill
- Drill bit (size will vary)
- Wood finish (optional)

Pattern on page 125

Using a Pruning Saw

If this is your first time using your saw, go slow! A pruning saw comes extremely sharp, and if you don't have a sense of what it will do, you can easily cut yourself with it. Keep your supporting hand about 2" (5.1cm) away from the blade and be mindful that, until you create a deep enough groove, the blade can easily hop out of its kerf and chatter to the side. Keep your strokes gentle at first to avoid this.

1 **Find and harvest the wood.** Go for a walk with your saw and scan the trees around you for branch crotches that might be the right size and shape for what you need. When you find something that works, cut it to size while still attached, if possible, and remove the piece from the tree as your final cut. This will be easier but might not be possible if the piece you want is out of reach, requiring you to cut lower down to drop it.

2 **Split your wood.** Place the edge of your axe on the cut end of the main section that will go against the wall and lift and tap down both axe and wood together on the stump to split off the back of the coat hook. This is called a bump cut.

The Bump Cut

The bump cut is a crucial technique. You never want to swing the axe down at the end grain of a chunk of wood, primarily because your other hand is probably somewhere in the vicinity holding the wood. Even if you miss your hand, you will very likely miss the mark you intend to hit. Instead, place the axe on the mark, lift both it and the wood together, and bring both down together to start a split. Never hold the wood below the axe, but always to the side.

3 **Create a flat spot.** Roughly flatten the back of the hook with the axe. It doesn't need to be perfectly flat, but it should rest solidly against a flat surface without wobbling.

4 **Remove the bark.** De-bark the rest of the coat hook using your sloyd knife and a series of squeeze cuts. This is the main grip used for spoon carving and is a perfect way to learn and practice the technique.

5 **Once you have the bark off, use squeeze cuts to facet the ends of the piece.** This can be simply chamfering the edges, or you can opt to carve the ends entirely. Drill several pilot holes for screws and treat the piece with whatever you have decided to use. You're done!

The Squeeze Cut

Squeeze cuts are created by opening and closing the fingers of the hand holding the wood and transferring that movement to the blade by bracing the thumb of that hand against the spine of the knife. The knife hand controls the angle of the blade (and therefore the depth of the cut) and sometimes pivots the blade forward by pulling back on the knife handle, but all the power comes from this opening and closing of the other hand. This gives tremendous power and almost total control. It is safe around other people and yourself.

Butter Knife

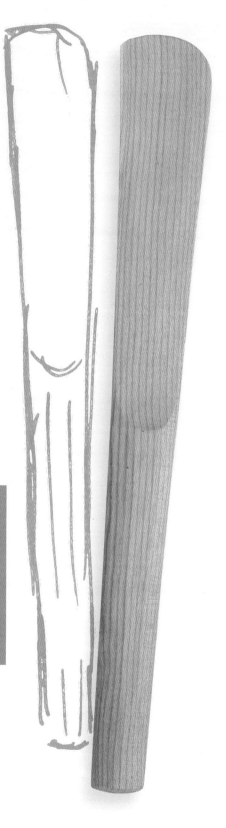

Approximate length: 9¾" (24.7cm)

A butter knife or spreader is the
perfect early project, but it can
also be quite challenging. Choose
a simple piece of wood, and
recognize that you are unlikely to
get the surfaces perfectly smooth
on your first attempt.

Tools and Materials
- Wood
- Axe
- Club
- Handsaw
- Sloyd knife
- Wood finish (optional)

Pattern on page 122

1 **Split the wood.** Start with a piece of wood several inches longer than the length of the butter knife you want. It will help tremendously if it is straight and free of knots. Use an axe and club to split the piece down, then use your axe to create a clean surface on one side. Hold the wood with just the tip of your thumb and your fingers tucked in behind. Use the extra length of the billet to stay away from your fingers with the axe. With each blow, lean down into the wood so that the face you are creating crosses the grain at a shallow angle.

2 **Outline the butter knife shape.** Draw your shape onto the axed face, with the butter knife's blade on the thinner side. In general, you want the centerline of your shape to line up with the grain and the actual outline to cross the grain at all times. Having the outline of the shape lined up with the grain will make it more difficult to determine which direction to make the cut in that spot.

Splitting with a Club

Splitting chunks of wood down to size with a club is the first step to most spoon carving projects, so it's important to know how to do it safely. The main thing is to make sure the axe handle is pointing off toward the side, NOT toward yourself. That way, when the club propels the axe down through the wood, it is heading off toward the side and not toward your leg. One other thing: sooner or later you will find yourself trying to split a piece of wood that doesn't want to split, usually because of a knot. It is crucial to identify this situation early on and extricate your axe before it becomes so lodged in the wood that you cannot free it without breaking the handle. If it does become stuck, your best bet is using a chainsaw to cut as close to the axe head as you dare, which will remove most of the squeezing power of the wood on the tool.

3 **Trim the wood to size.** Use a saw to remove the excess wood on both ends of the form. Some people like to do this with the axe, but that is easy to mess up and can cause microtears in the end grain of the wood if the axe isn't sharp enough (or the wood is slightly punky). Whenever I am sawing, I like to sink my axe into the stump and then brace the wood against it.

Bracing a Billet for Sawing

Anyone who has tried to simply hold a piece of wood down and saw it knows how frustrating that is. It's far better to sink your axe into the far side of the stump then place the billet so that the end to be cut is sticking just slightly over the edge of the stump, your hand is leaning your weight down on the middle section, and the other end of the billet is tucked up against the heel of the axe head. When you use the saw now, it pulls on the wood, your hand creates a pivot point, and the axe prevents the billet from spinning.

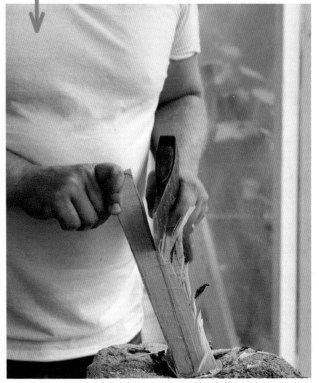

4 **Axe the outline.** Start from the widest part of the form and go to the narrowest.

Bagging Your Work

Carving wood is all about controlling its moisture content. Once you start to work it, the wood can dry out quickly, becoming difficult to carve. In as little as five minutes, a skin of air-hardened wood can form on the outer surface of a piece that bogs you down, slowing the carving process, so that by the time you get to any given surface, it has already become hardened and slows you down further. The faster you can carve, the easier the carving will be. Short of that, it pays to keep cycling through the surfaces, continuously getting down underneath any hardened surfaces. And any time you stop carving, even if for just a few minutes, wrap the piece in a plastic bag. It doesn't need to be sealed or tight; a regular produce bag wrapped around it will do.

5 **Axe the back of the form.** Use bump cuts to remove material at the end of the form. Then, continue axing down the face, at first being extremely gentle and cautious when you are near the thumb that is pinning the wood down. Use increasing force as you drive the cut deeper. When you are done axing your blank, wrap it in a plastic bag if you are not going to carve it immediately.

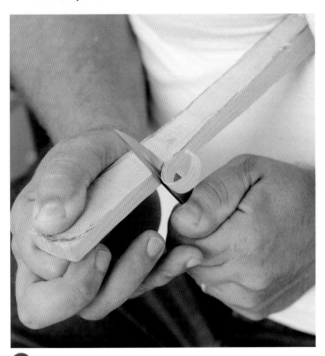

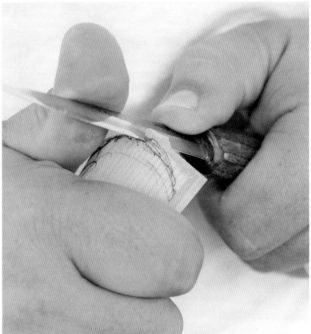

6 **Carve the outline.** Using pull cuts, carve down the sides of the butter knife blade. Then, switch to squeeze cuts to get the bit that is too close to your body.

7 **Carve the ends.** Shape the ends of the form using squeeze cuts. On the butter knife blade end, try to create one smooth curve with as few cuts as possible.

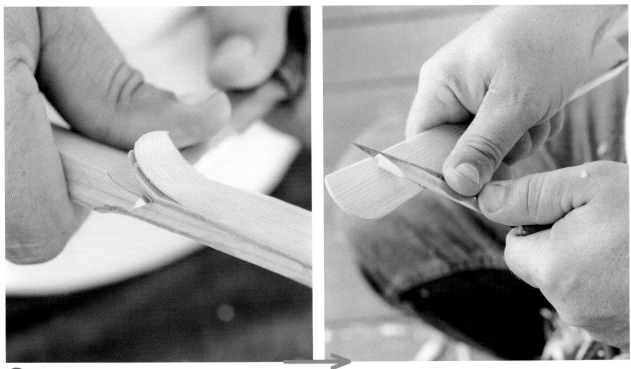

8 **Create the transition between the handle and blade.** Decide where the handle/blade transition starts and use the tip of the knife to lean down into the grain there. Scooch your hand along and use squeeze cuts to carve from there to the end of the blade.

9 **Facet the handle using pull cuts.** Feel out which way the grain wants to run. Just a slight tip of the form within the grain can send it one way or the other.

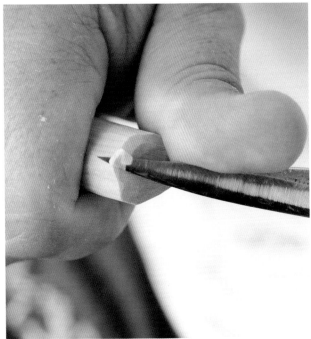

10 **Facet the handle end.** Use squeeze cuts to facet the end of the handle. Burnish and finish, then put it to use!

Honey Dipper

Approximate length 8¾" (22.2cm)

A honey dipper is a nice stepping-stone to larger forms because the attention to detail needed to create this radially symmetrical form is good practice for the decisions you'll be making later. While the classic honey dipper has grooves to hold more honey, this design opts for clean, hexagonal faces to make it simple to carve. Plus, it looks good standing on your counter!

Tools and Materials
- Wood
- Axe
- Club
- Pruning saw
- Sloyd knife
- Hook knife
- Wood finish (optional)

Pattern on page 122

1 **Create a flat face on your wood.** Having split a piece of wood down to roughly the size you want, axe a flat face into one side of it. Lean your cut into the wood so that the created face crosses the grain just slightly.

2 **Create the outline.** Draw the outline of the honey dipper on this face, keeping the shape away from any end grain that might have cracks in it and otherwise avoiding any problem areas you can identify.

3 **Trim the ends.** Saw the ends of the form right to the line you have defined.

4 **Shape the billet.** Axe the billet into a square, or as close to it as you can, again leaning into each face to create a slight taper to the resulting blank. Be careful not to cut into the outline you've created.

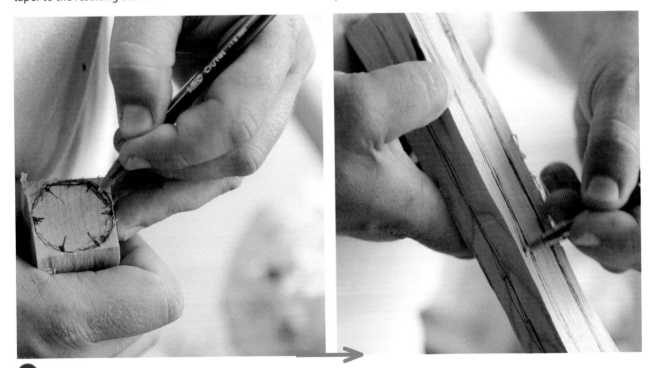

5 **Create the hexagon outline.** On each end, draw the circle that represents the width of the form where it meets that end grain. On the handle end, this is quite small. On the other end, the circle should fill the square. Then, place six dots evenly around the circumference of this larger circle and connect the dots between each circle to define the material to be removed.

6 **Shape the hexagon.** Axe new faces to the blank that match each of the faces of this hexagon, doing your best to keep them the same size as they taper. It doesn't need to be perfect, though, particularly once you get past the point of the handle transition.

7 **Create the handle transition.** Axe in the handle transition with a series of gentle blows. This is more about defining the point of transition than it is about creating the exact shape you want with the axe. You'll do that with the knife in a minute.

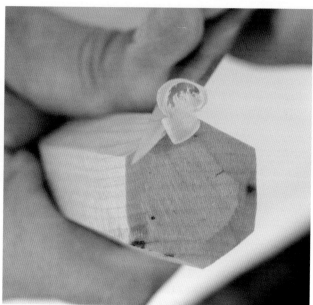

8 **Clean up the hexagon faces.** Switching to the sloyd knife, clean up each of the hexagon faces with a series of pull cuts. Try to maintain the taper and relative size of each face in relationship to the others.

9 **Define the handle transition.** Using a series of squeeze cuts coupled with a twisting motion, define the handle transition. Be careful not to go too deep at first.

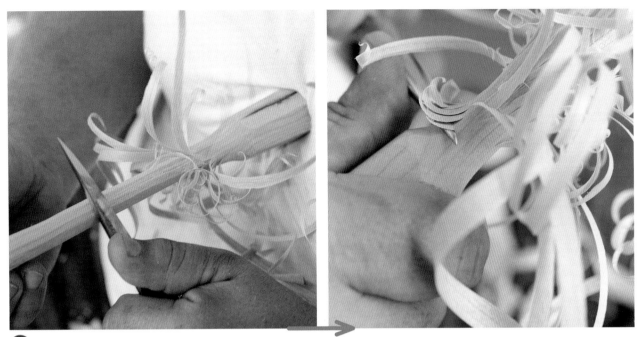

10 **Thin the handle and chamfer the end.** Thin the handle with a series of pull cuts coming from the other direction. Leave these cuts attached all around, and when you have the handle the thickness you want, clean them up by coming in from the first direction with more hand squeeze cuts, using just the tip of the blade and being careful to get just barely under the pull cuts. Chamfer the end of the handle with a series of squeeze cuts.

11 **Create a hollow.** Using the hook knife, hollow the end of the honey dipper. Leave a rim around the edge, but otherwise remove the center material. This will help the dipper stand without wobbling, and it will also help it hold more honey when in use.

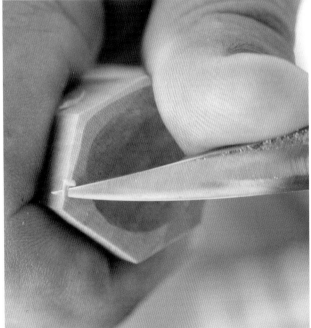

12 **Chamfer the hollow.** Using a series of squeeze cuts, chamfer the hollowed end of the dipper. Polish and wax the form and that's it!

Simple Spatula

Approximate length: 8¾" (22.2cm)

This spatula is probably the most-used utensil in our kitchen—which is great because it's also one of the easiest forms to make! Beware making the blade too wide; it becomes exponentially more difficult to carve the wider it gets.

Tools and Materials
- Wood
- Axe
- Club
- Pruning saw
- Sloyd knife
- Wood finish (optional)

Pattern on page 122

Ma's Pie Crust

...lt
...ter

ice water
white vinegar

makes top + bottom
450 for 10 min
350 for 35-45 min

Sweet Hot Salad

Sour Cream

...water
1 Tbsp Oil
food coloring

Stir flour int...

Blade End

Handle End

2 **Draw your shape onto the crank face.** Orient the form so the blade just beyond the neck is at the bottom of the V.

1 **Create a crank face.** Split a billet that is a couple of inches longer than you need, a little wider than you need, and relatively thin. You'll start by axing in what is called a crank face. A crank face is a very shallow V that establishes the line of the handle and the line of the top of the bowl of a spoon or, in this case, the blade of the spatula. Start on the blade end and drive a line down with the axe, beginning several inches away from the hand holding the billet. These several inches are critical to keep your hand safe and will be trimmed off in a bit. Remember to tilt the billet so the axe can remain straight up and down, and never let the edge of the axe come up over your hand. Then, drive the line down on the handle side. The bottom of the V does not need to be perfect. It is easy to make this too deep by chasing a needlessly perfect surface.

3 **Trim the ends and create a stop cut.** Trim both ends of the blank, and then make a stop cut at the neck detail.

Stop Cuts

A stop cut is a saw cut made at the neck of a spoon that prevents the wood being split from the handle from cracking into the bowl. Some stop cuts are on the far side of the form and can be made as usual, but ones on the same side of the form as yourself are most easily made by rotating the hand holding the saw (without changing how you are gripping it) so your palm faces out.

4 **Thin the back of the blank.** Use the axe to drive a line from the deepest point of the V (a point we will call the crank going forward) to the tip of the blade, and then from the crank to the end of the handle. This will keep the crank point the thickest and taper the handle and blade away from it. As you drive this cut down, pry the axe sideways after each blow or two to reduce the binding pressure of the wood being removed.

6 **Use pop cuts when you near the stop cut.** When approaching the stop cut while axing the handle, use pop cuts to keep from splitting the blade of the spatula. To make pop cuts, tilt the blank further over than normal and make a series of chops about 1½" (3.8cm) from the stop cut and 1½" (3.8cm) apart. It will take a bit of practice, but you will be able to calibrate the force of these chops to send a shock wave through the grain, popping the chunk of wood out to the stop cut at the depth of the chop. Finish driving the line of the handle down to where you made the pop cuts, being very careful near your hand when you start them. Finally, axe the other side from the blade all the way down the handle. You may find it helpful to make relief cuts up from the bottom before driving this line down (see next step).

5 **Axe to the outline.** Go from the widest point to the narrowest point. In this case, that means from the tip of the blade to the neck, then from the end of the handle to the neck.

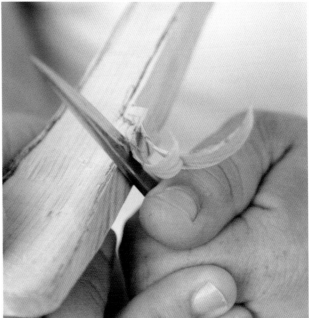

8 **Carve the outline.** Switch to the sloyd knife and begin carving the outline around the tip of the blade with a series of squeeze cuts. Then using a series of pull cuts, carve down the sides of the blade and handle. Trim the handle end with squeeze cuts. On the side without the stop cut, you might get away with a pull cut all the way from the blade down the handle in one direction, depending on how the form is oriented with the grain. Otherwise, you will need to negotiate the grain change on both sides.

7 **Thin the back of the handle.** To continue thinning, use a series of relief cuts. Relief cuts are a series of chops made from the bottom of the handle to about halfway up, spaced an inch or so apart, whose purpose is to break up the wood fibers. Once the relief cuts are made, it should be easy to drive a line down the back of the handle. Without the relief cuts, your axe would get stuck about halfway down, as the depth of the cut would overcome the axe's wedging force.

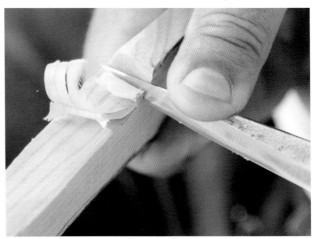

9 **Clean up the neck.** To clean up the neck of the form, leave some pull cuts attached at the neck and come in from the opposite direction. On the stop cut side, this is done with a squeeze cut and a twisting motion with the tip of the knife. On the other side, use a pull cut to go all the way from the blade down to the handle end.

⑩ Dress the top face of the spatula blade. To do this, use a series of pull cuts. Start by defining the line of the edge that you want at a shallow angle, then work down the top of the blade in a series of narrow strips, retaining a bit of camber to the top. A cross section of the blade should be thin at the edges and slightly thicker in the middle. Leave these pull cuts attached.

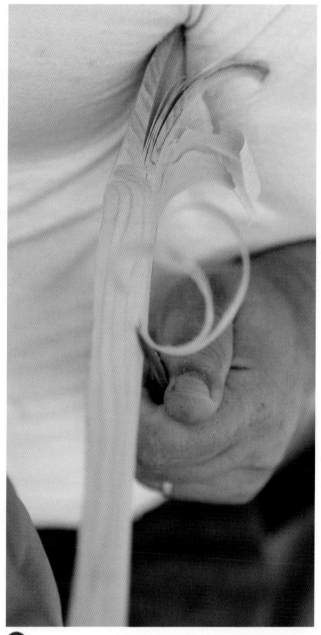

⑪ Dress the handle and the back of the blade. Make a series of pull cuts on the top of the handle, then come in with a strong squeeze cut from the neck to get underneath them and clean this up. You usually won't be able to get this perfect, so call it good before you ruin it. Then, dress the back of the blade with a series of strong squeeze cuts, using the base of the blade and pivoting it against your thumb to continue each cut as long as possible. Define the edges first, then work the surface in a series of strips, maintaining a camber. Dress the back of the handle with pull cuts for the first half. Dress the end of the handle by bracing the knife in your fist against your knee and pulling the wood back against the blade.

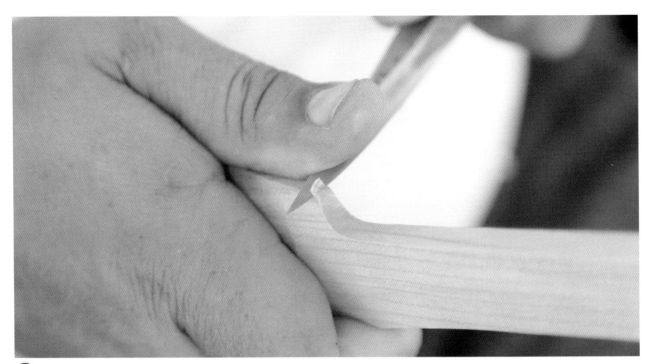

⑫ Round the blade corners. Ease the corners of the blade tip and shoulder with some careful squeeze cuts, aiming for a nicely rounded outline.

⑬ Create the handle facets. Pull facets down the top of the handle from the end to the blade, being careful as you reach the neck to not dig in too deep. If you do this with enough control, the neck detail can take on a lovely curve. I tend to pull one strong facet to knock off the original corner, then a more delicate one for each of the new corners it creates. Pull a delicate facet on the sides of the blade, then use a squeeze cut to create a microfacet on the blade edge. Flip the form over and facet the back of the handle in the same way. Use squeeze cuts to facet the handle end. Polish, wax, and enjoy!

Baking Spatula

Approximate length: 11½" (29.2cm)

While it might seem like this form is easier to carve than the simple spatula, it is not. Forms that incorporate any amount of crank have much more predictable grain flow, as the form leans across the grain of the wood everywhere. Here, the struggle will be to carve something that follows the grain, which will force you to read what the wood is willing to do and sometimes reverse the direction you are cutting to clean up a section. You can vastly simplify this project by using the straightest, clearest bit of wood you have.

Tools and Materials
- Wood
- Axe
- Club
- Pruning saw
- Sloyd knife
- Wood finish (optional)

Pattern on page 123

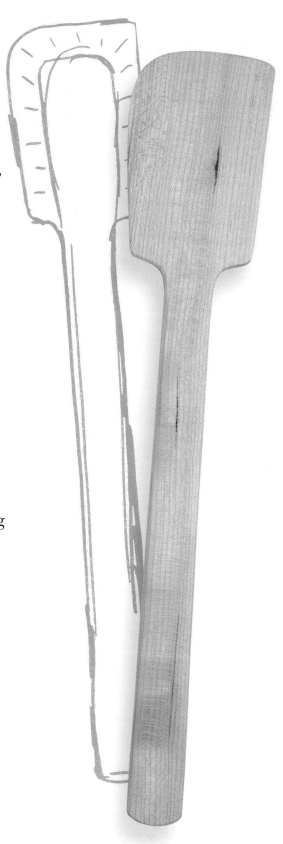

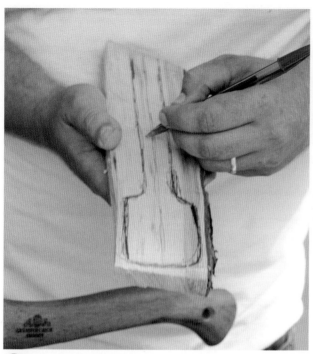

1 **Draw the outline.** Following the same procedure as usual, split your billet and axe in a clean face. Then, draw the outline of the spatula, taking care to line the handle up with the grain as much as possible.

2 **Trim the ends and make your stop cuts.** Note that the stop cuts are not right up against the outline but are kept ¼"–½" (6.4–12.7mm) away. This gives you a more forgiving target when it comes time to axe out this material.

3 **Split the waste off the handle.** Place the axe on the end grain right at the outline and tap the axe and blank down on the stump together to start the split. Be mindful that the split will run toward the side with less mass, so you might need to do this in stages to keep the split from running into the handle, depending on the width of your billet.

5 **Axe the back of the blank.** Lean into the grain enough to create a slight taper to the form. The handle should be the thickest part and the blade end should be the thinnest.

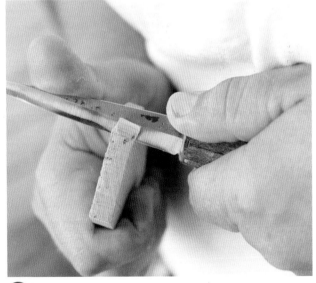

4 **Clear the neck and axe the outline.** Use pop cuts to clear the material at the neck. Remember to start 1½" (3.8cm) back from the stop cut and to tilt your blank over so that the axe edge is never pointing at the shoulder of the form. Use enough force to send that shock wave through the wood, popping it free. Finish removing the material with standard axe blows, driving the line down from the handle end, easing up as you approach the area already cleared by the pop cuts. You don't want to come through with so much momentum that the axe carries through and taps the shoulder of the form. Even if this doesn't split it immediately, it will create a stress fracture that will open as the wood dries out. Axe the outline of the blade, from the blade tip down to the shoulders on either side, and then just a little around the rounded bit of the blade. Don't try to get this close; it is easier and more accurate to simply cut it with the knife.

6 **Carve the outline.** Switching to the sloyd knife, carve the outline of the spatula, starting with a squeeze cut to trim around the rounded corner of the blade. Try to get this with just one or two cuts, as this will create a cleaner line.

7 **Carve and dress the spatula.** Use a similar long squeeze cut to carve across the tip of the spatula. If it is too thick for you to do this easily, use the axe to thin the back of the blade some more. You want it to be about ¼" (6.4mm) thick. Finish carving the outline with pull cuts on the blade and handle and squeeze cuts on the shoulder and handle end. Dress the front and back sides with pull cuts on the handle and pivoting squeeze cuts on the blade. Remember that there is no crank, so the squeeze cuts on the blade go from the handle to the blade tip on both sides. The only exception is if the grain has a lean to it. Then, you should cut in the direction that allows the blade to leave a clean surface.

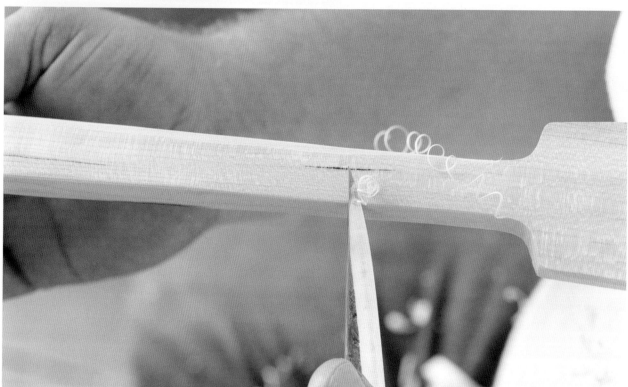

8 **Add microchamfers.** Pull long microchamfers on the handle. I like to make two microchamfers to each corner, which significantly softens it without rounding it as much. Other than the microchamfers, be sure to leave your handle rectangular. Use squeeze cuts to facet the end of the handle.

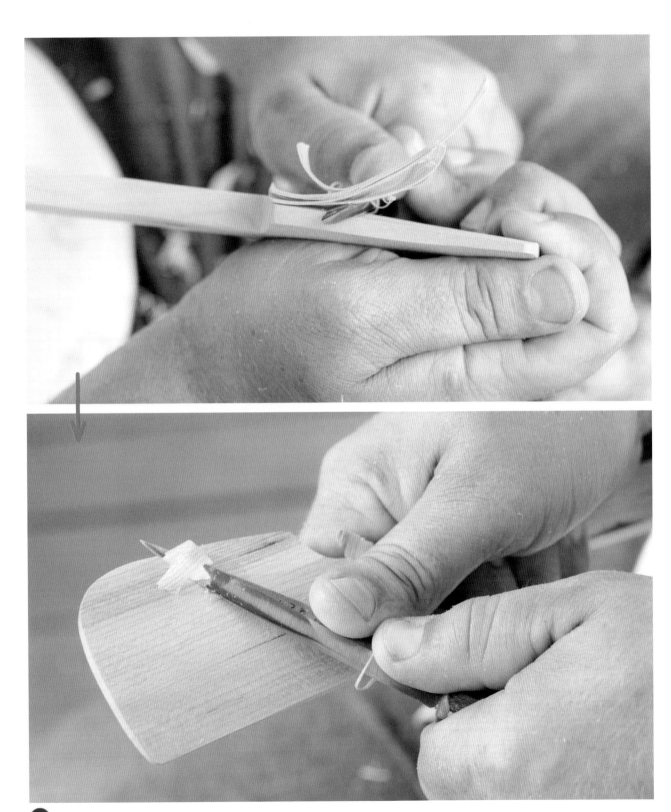

9 **Carve blade facets.** Create the big, defining facet on one or both sides of the blade using a combination of pull or squeeze cuts, depending on grain flow. Maintain an even edge thickness and soften both sides of the edge with microchamfers. Polish and wax the spatula and you're done!

Pot Scraper

Approximate length: 4" (10.2cm)

This form is a good way to learn how to use the hook knife because it will automatically teach you to work in the palm of your hand, there being nothing else to hold onto. This is an important habit to develop, as it gives you much more power and control over the hook knife.

Tools and Materials

- Wood
- Axe
- Club
- Pruning saw
- Sloyd knife
- Hook knife
- Wood finish (optional)

Pattern on page 124

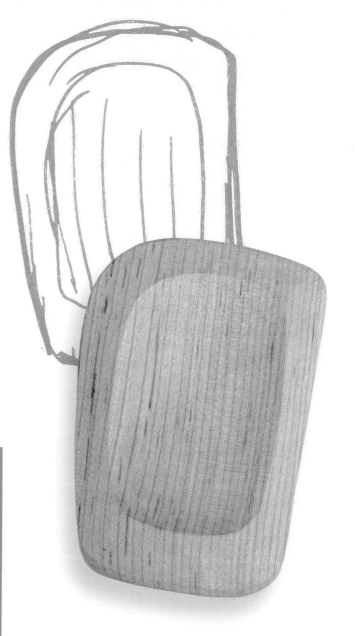

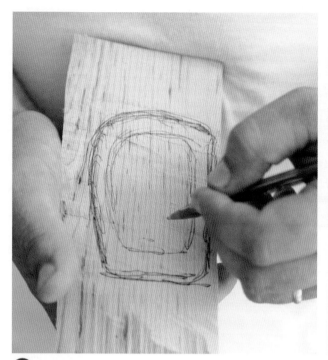

1 **Axe out a clean face and draw the outline.** This form is easiest started on a billet two or three times the length of the finished piece.

2 **Axe out the back face.** Create a slight taper toward the working edge.

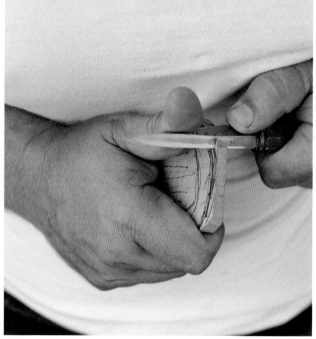

3 **Trim the billet.** Pin the billet against the stump and the back of the axe and trim the working end, then saw the form from the rest of the billet.

4 **Carve the outline.** Use squeeze cuts and a few very tight pull cuts to carve the outline. When working this close to your body with pull cuts, make sure your forearm is pinned tight to your chest to control the potential reach of the knife. Whenever possible, use squeeze cuts.

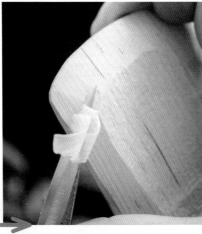

5 **Draw the edge borders and carve facets.** Use a pencil to draw the borders of the edge you want to create, and then use a series of squeeze cuts to facet all four sides on the front and back to this mark. Try to give the facets the same angle on each side, but don't worry about the width of the facet. That will be controlled by the hollow, coming next.

6 **Create a hollow.** Use a pencil to draw the extent of the hollow you want to make on each side, then begin removing material with the hook knife. Make sure you are all the way choked up on the hook knife blade, with the spine of the blade against your forefinger. Brace your thumb on the edge of the piece and pull the blade toward your thumb, stopping before you reach it. If you aren't choked up on the blade, you will eventually cut yourself.

7 **Cut with the grain.** Hollow across the grain initially, then switch to cuts with the grain. If the hook doesn't want to exit a cut, twist the blade against the wood (or rotate the hand holding the piece, which achieves the same thing) to release it.

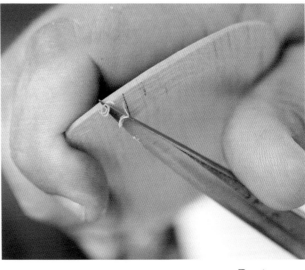

8 **Create microchamfers.** Run microchamfers around all the working edges, as small as you can. If they are too big, they will keep the scraper from doing its job. The tiniest of microchamfers will make the edge last longer. Polish and wax and start using it!

Pie Server

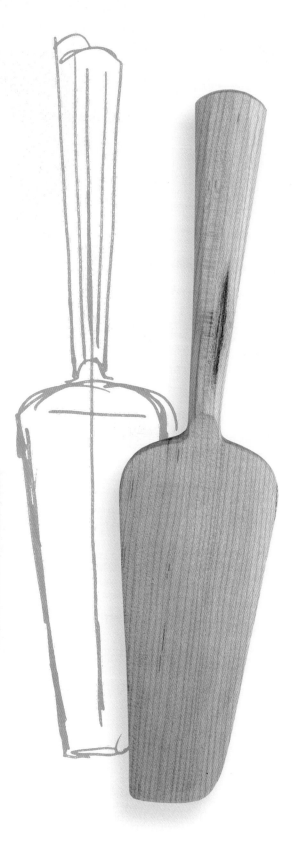

Approximate length: 10" (25.4cm)

This pie server nicely pushes the boundaries of the previous couple of forms, as it is more delicate and has more flat surface area. Choose your piece of wood wisely, making sure it has a clear, straight grain.

Tools and Materials
- Wood
- Axe
- Club
- Pruning saw
- Sloyd knife
- Wood finish (optional)

Pattern on page 123

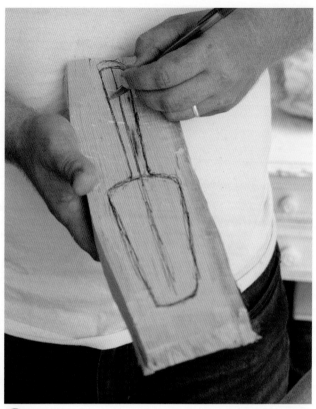

1 **Create the crank face.** As usual, start by axing in the crank face. But, in this case, make the arms of the V equal in length to accommodate the long blade of the server.

2 **Draw the outline.** Make sure to orient the shoulders of the form at the bottom of the V. This placement will be crucial for negotiating the grain change later.

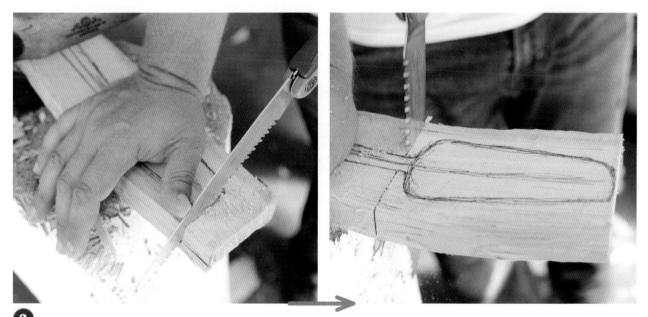

3 **Trim and make stop cuts.** Trim the ends of the blank and make stop cuts on either side of the neck, back ½" (1.3cm) from the outline itself.

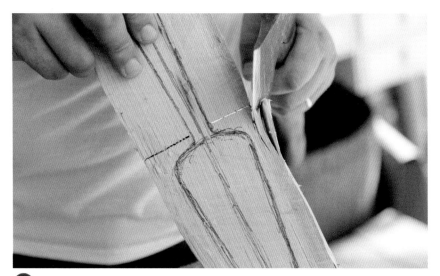

4 **Axe in the blade end outline.** Be careful not to dig in too deeply.

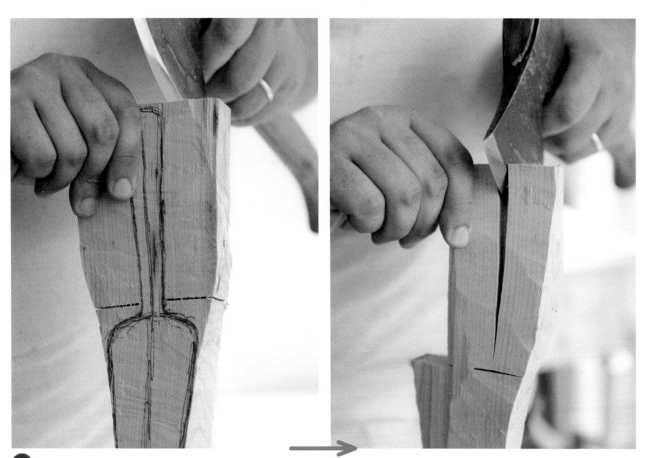

5 **Split the waste material off the handle.** Use bump cuts and pop cuts, then drive the line down to the outline. Flip the form around and place the neck/shoulder transition on the edge of the stump so the handle of the server is hanging over the edge and the shoulder is on top of the stump. Axe very gently around the shoulder outline. This is why you keep the stop cuts back from the outline. You need material here to be able to get your range with the first axe blows without ruining things. Don't try to get this perfect, though; just make it good enough to finish with the knife.

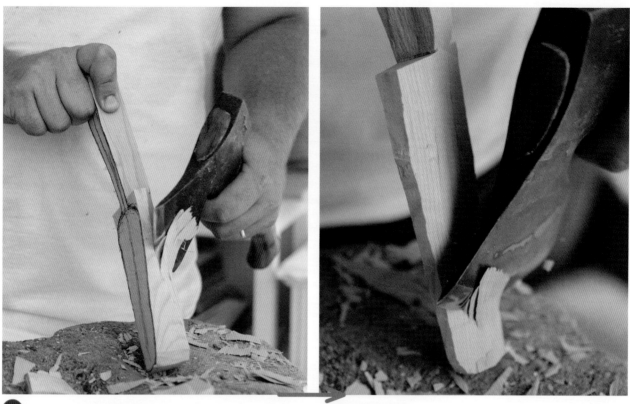

6 **Thin the form.** Thin the back of blade with the axe, then thin the back of the handle.

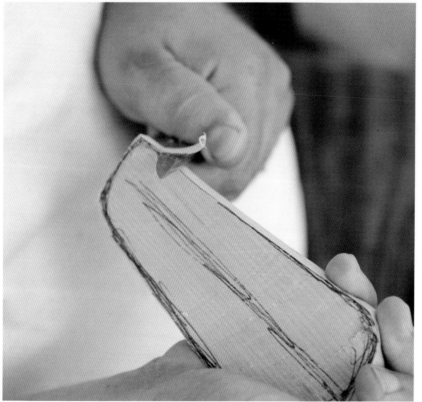

7 **Carve the blade outline.**
Switching to the sloyd knife, use a pull cut to carve the outline of the pie server blade, pinning your knife wrist to your chest when you get as close to yourself as you can. Then, keeping your knife wrist pinned, pull the pie server straight out away from you to finish the cut (so it switches from the knife moving to the form moving). This is called a chest brace cut.

8 **Use pull cuts to cut the handle outline.** Leave the wood slivers attached at the neck, then use squeeze cuts to carve up and around the shoulder and get just under the attached pull cuts. This should leave the neck clean. Remember, if your knife can't do this, it's time to sharpen, paying particular attention to the tip of the blade.

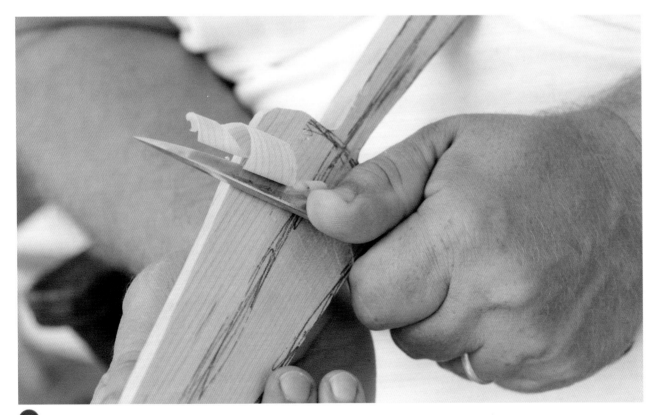

9 **Clean up the blade face with pull cuts.** Start at the edges to define them first. Leave these attached as they approach the shoulder area.

10 **Carve the handle.** Then, create the bump down, which is done with a powerful squeeze cut that scoops down from the top of the handle to the level of the pull cuts and eases just underneath them.

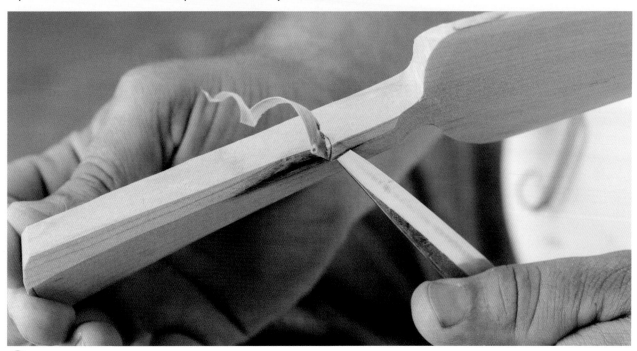

11 **Pull chamfers down the handle.** When you get close to the bump down cut, ease the chamfers so they make a nice arch. Add microchamfers to the edges of the blade and facet the end of the handle.

12 **Thin the back of the blade.** Use a series of powerful squeeze cuts with an extra pivot at the end to give them as much length as possible. Define the edges first, then thin down the middle.

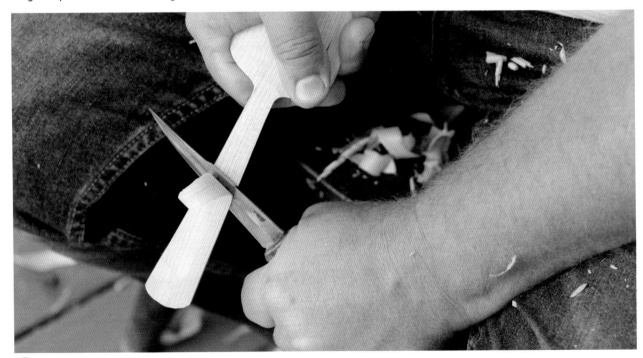

13 **Dress the back of the handle.** First, use pull cuts. Then, follow with knee brace cuts, bracing the knife forearm on your knee and pull the form back against the blade. Chamfer the back of the handle with pull cuts that turn into chest brace cuts, then add microchamfers to all sharp edges. Polish and wax, then use!

Cooking Spoon

Approximate length: 11" (27.9cm)

This cooking spoon is a great next project because its fat handle and relatively small bowl make it forgiving and easy to carve. Keep the amount of crank minimal, just enough to make the carving direction certain.

Tools and Materials
- Wood
- Axe
- Club
- Pruning saw
- Sloyd knife
- Hook knife
- Wood finish (optional)

Pattern on page 124

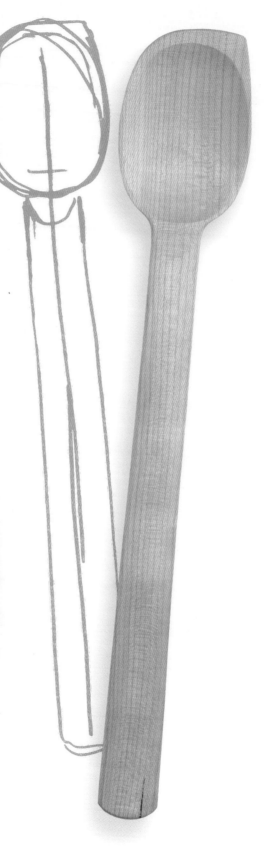

1 **Axe the crank into the billet.** Keep a couple of inches away from either end.

2 **Draw the outline.** Draw the bowl first, then draw the centerline. Continue the centerline down the handle. Tilt the billet away from you to foreshorten the perspective, which will allow you to see if this line veers to one side or the other. Then draw the handle outline.

3 **Trim the ends and make the usual stop cuts.** Practice getting your stop cuts right up to the outline but not over it. Pay attention to make the cuts straight up and down as you get to the line.

4 **Thin the back of the billet.** Use a series of axe blows to drive a line from the bottom of the crank to the tip, then from the bottom of the crank down the handle. Use relief cuts on the handle if necessary to keep the axe from binding.

5 **Remove the handle waste.** Use pop cuts to remove the handle waste near the stop cuts. Then, use bump cuts to start removing the side waste on the handle, and drive the line down to where the pop cuts left off.

7 **Axe the bowl's shoulders.** Place the shoulder against the edge of the stump with the handle hanging over the edge. Be very gentle with this. Thin down the back of the handle one more time, using relief cuts if needed to keep the axe from binding.

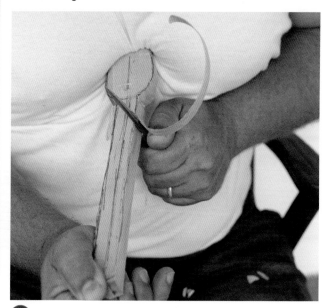

6 **Axe the back of the bowl again.** This time, lower the handle of the spoon so the axe creates the curve of the back of the bowl. Do one set that defines the bottom of the bowl, then one on each side that creates the curve of the bowl from side to side. Use bump cuts to remove side material from the bowl outline, then axe around the front of the bowl, avoiding recutting the wood directly across the end grain.

8 **Carve the outline.** Switch to the to the sloyd knife and cut to the drawn outline using pull cuts and squeeze cuts. Keep these cuts at 90 degrees to the top face of the spoon. You do not need to get the outline perfect at this stage. Just get underneath any axe and saw marks so there are no surprises later on.

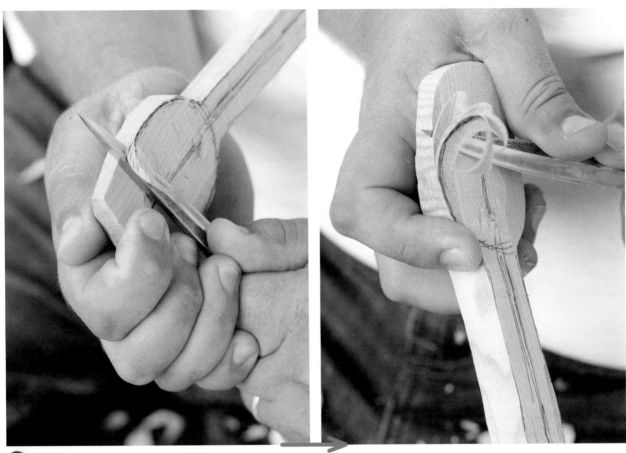

9 **Dress the bowl's face.** For this, you will need to use two forms of pivot cuts (see sidebar below).

Rim Pivot Cuts

Pivot Cut 1: Pin the spoon against your sternum with your hand on the bowl tip and press the spine of the knife against the tips of these fingers. This is your pivot point. Keep your thumb tucked under the spoon. With your knife wrist held stiff, lift your knife elbow, pivoting the blade down toward yourself. This way, you can apply a lot of force while being safe because the force is applied away from you but is then transformed into force toward yourself by the pivot action. This is not a pull cut! Using this pivot cut, you can dress the entire rim of one side of the spoon bowl.

Pivot Cut 2: Hold the neck of the spoon between your pointer and middle fingers, with the handle sticking out away from you. Tuck the tip of the bowl into the base of your thumb. Now, place the spine of the knife against the tip of your thumb. That is your pivot point. Keep your thumb fully extended. Do not let it bend, but shift your whole thumb from side to side to change the placement of the blade. Pulling the blade back against your thumb, pivot the handle toward yourself, which will pivot the blade away from you. Again, the force is applied in the opposite direction the knife edge is pointing, pulling the spine of the blade back against your thumb, and the force is redirected by the pivoting action. Stop halfway through this side of the bowl rim and shift your ring finger to the other side of the neck, then finish cutting that side of the rim.

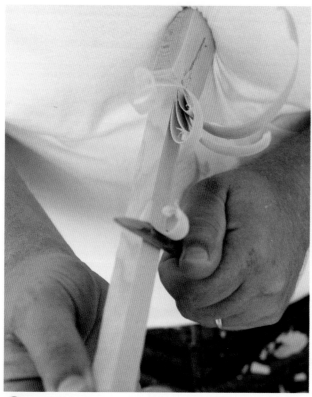

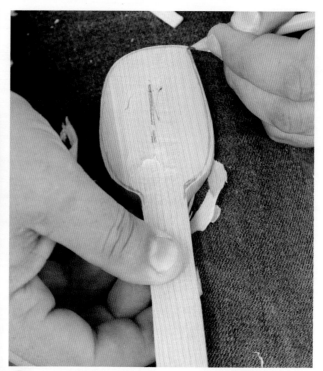

10 **Dress the handle and back of the spoon.** Dress the top of the handle with a pull cut. Then, dress the back of the spoon using the usual pull cuts, knee brace cuts, and squeeze cuts. The goal is to clean up the lines while reducing the rim thickness by about half.

11 **Redraw the outline with a sharp pencil.** Keep the heel of your hand pinned to the tabletop or your knee and draw arcs with your hand while pivoting the spoon. This will allow you to draw much more consistent curves than if you simply tried to draw the shape. For the straight lines of the handle, rest your hand on a surface and slide it straight toward yourself.

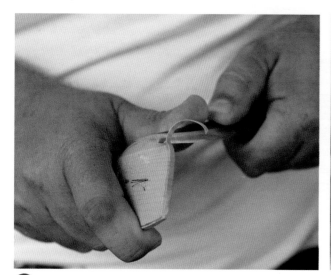

12 **Recut the new outline.** Repeat all the previous steps regarding cutting the outline. Then, recut the top and bottom. Again, reduce the rim thickness by half. Using a squeeze cut, create a bump down at the neck.

13 **Chamfer the handle.** Use pull cuts on the top and pull cuts followed by chest brace cuts on the back. Facet the end of the handle.

14 **Create a hollow.** Switching to the hook knife, roughly hollow the bowl, starting in the middle and making the hollow wider as you go deeper. Cradle the bowl in the palm of your hand. Pinch the handle between your thumb and forefinger, and remember to choke up on the blade. Go about three quarters of the way.

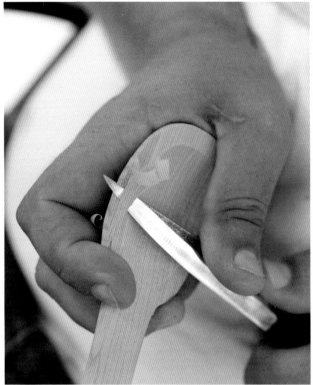

15 **Level the rim.** Use one more series of pivot cuts, this time getting the knife as flat to the top surface as you can. Before, these cuts were always at a shallow angle to avoid the need to cut all the material in the center of the bowl. Clean up the bump, if necessary, with the tip of the knife.

16 **Finish the bowl.** Returning to the hook, establish the line of the inner rim with a series of cuts that trace around the edge. Then, make a series of strong cuts from the tip of the bowl down to the grain change, pinning the handle against your chest and supporting the bottom of the bowl with the heel of your hand. Start each cut right at the line of the inner rim. Finally, finish the bowl with some cuts in the back shoulders of the bowl that start in the neck at the middle and go out to the sides, being careful not to let these dig in so deep that they catch the grain. Using the sloyd knife, cut microchamfers around the bowl on the top and underside of the rim. Polish and wax the spoon and it's ready to use!

Serving Spoon

Approximate length: 10¾" (27.3cm)

Now that you have a proper
spoon under your belt, it's time
to tackle something with a larger
bowl size and a more challenging
handle shape.

Tools and Materials
- Wood
- Axe
- Club
- Pruning saw
- Sloyd knife
- Hook knife
- Wood finish (optional)

Pattern on page 124

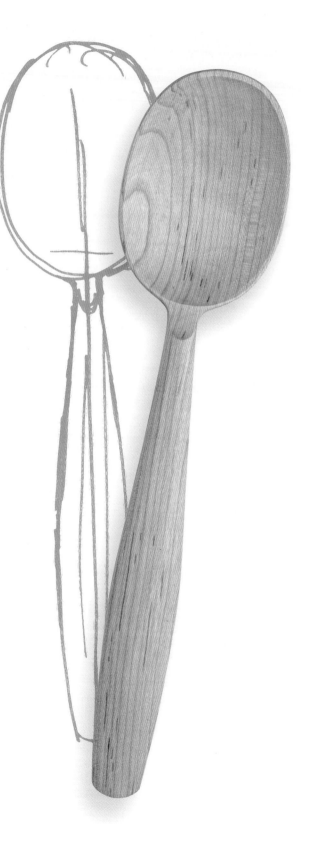

1 **Draw the outline.** Use a billet that has been split down to size and had the crank face axed in. Trim the ends and make the stop cuts. Keep them back from the outline by a ½" (1.3cm).

2 **Thin the billet and make pop cuts.** Reduce the thickness of the billet on the back, if needed, then make pop cuts at the neck.

3 **Axe the outline.** Because of the reverse taper on the handle, you can't do bump down cuts to remove the handle material. Instead, flip the spoon around and axe from the middle of the handle down to the handle end. Axe around the outline of the front of the bowl, staying back from the bit right in the middle where it's pure end grain.

4 **Axe the curve into the back of the bowl.** Lower the spoon handle as you drive the line from the bottom of the crank to the tip of the bowl. Axe out the sides of the back of the bowl, as well.

5 **Axe around the shoulders of the bowl.** Start at the widest point of the bowl and drive around the curve until you get close to the neck. Remember to support the neck on the edge of the stump. Finally, thin down the back of the handle, starting at the deepest part of the crank on the bowl and using relief cuts toward the bottom of the handle, if needed. You do this last to keep the neck as strong as possible for the shoulder cuts, as the force of the blows exerts a tremendous amount of shearing force on the neck, even if properly supported.

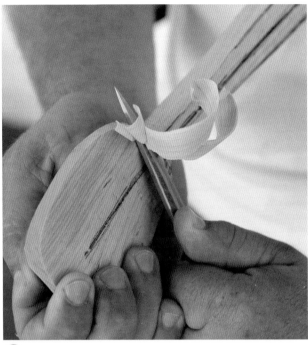

6 **Rough out the outline of the spoon.** Using the sloyd knife, conduct the usual sequence of squeeze cuts for the bowl and pull cuts for the handle. You might find a knee brace cut or a squeeze cut helpful to handle the reverse taper of the handle. Remember that the purpose of roughing out the spoon is mostly to get down below axe and saw marks, and only secondarily to get the shape cleaned up. Moving fast is more important than getting the shape perfect at this stage.

7 **Dress the bowl rim.** Use pivot cuts to dress the line of the bowl rim. Pay attention to keeping your pivot point firmly connected and pivoting to create the force, rather than pushing or pulling the blade.

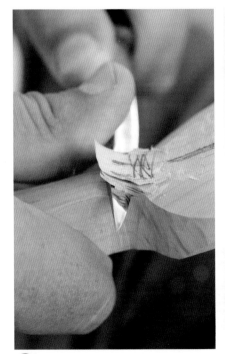

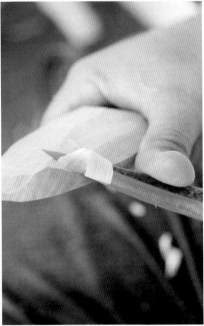

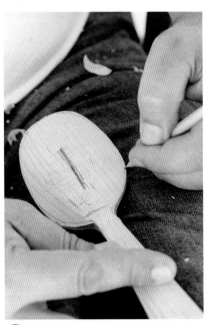

8 **Dress the top of the handle and create the bump.** Use the tip of the blade to create a tight little scallop. Create a bump down at the neck.

9 **Pull up the underside of the bowl rim.** Use a series of squeeze cuts, then rough out the rest of the back of the bowl. Dress the back of the handle with pull cuts and knee brace cuts.

10 **Redraw the outline.** Define the neck right away, then draw on whichever side of the bowl has less material. The side with more material will accommodate whatever you draw on the side with less.

11 **Recut the outline and add handle chamfers.** Get your outline as clean as possible, then pull handle chamfers on the top and bottom. Facet the handle end, then dress the rim again using pivot cuts. Recut the bump down to clean up its shape.

12 **Rough out the spoon bowl.** With the hook knife, start in the middle and dig it deeper from all different angles as it goes wider and deeper. It is always easiest to start with cuts going across the grain, but experiment with cuts that sweep around the edge of the hole you're creating. You can often get away with more dynamic cuts than you think once you remove the initial hump of material in the middle.

13 **Level the rim with pivot cuts.** Be careful not to snag the near side of the rim with the heel of the blade as you concentrate on your cut with the tip.

15 **Add microchamfers.** Cut microchamfers on the inner rim with the hook knife, then on the outer rim with the sloyd. When cutting the outer rim microchamfer, orient the knife parallel to the edge of the bowl. If it is angled more in line with the top rim, you will likely split the rim, as the blade will be digging into the grain.

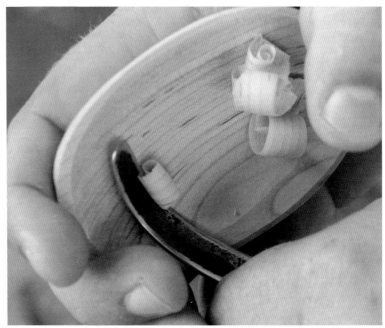

14 **Finish cutting the bowl.** First, define the inner rim, then cut straight down from the tip of the bowl into the center. Finish by scooping from the center of the shoulders back to the sides and gently clean up the grain change from whatever direction seems to be needed. Be careful not to dive deeper than your hook knife can negotiate. If your hook has only a shallow curve to it, keep cleaning up all the parts of the bowl and go down in layers so that when your knife starts bottoming out (which will be when the tip of the hook starts to dig in), you can be done.

16 **Thin the back of the bowl.** Use a series of squeeze cuts to thin the back of the bowl, starting at the rim and then smoothing the rest. Pay particular attention to the back of the shoulders, which are easy to leave unnecessarily thick. Take care not to remove too much from the back of the neck. Use your fingers to feel the cross section of the spoon bowl as you go. You want it thickest in the center and thinning to the edge. When you're happy with it, polish and wax the spoon. You're done!

Coffee Scoop

Approximate length: 5½" (14cm)

Small forms present the problem that they are hard to hold, and are potentially dangerous to axe out if you don't exercise extreme caution and keep your fingers out of harm's way. Interestingly, the trickiest thing is trying to trim the ends of such a short form and making stop cuts at the neck. The best way around this is to start with the blank attached to a longer billet, which gives you a more secure handhold as you saw it. These short forms are also a great chance to orient the object differently in the wood, such that there are concentric rings in the grain centered or off to the side of the bowl. This orientation is weaker than when the grain runs from end to end, but that doesn't matter for scoops.

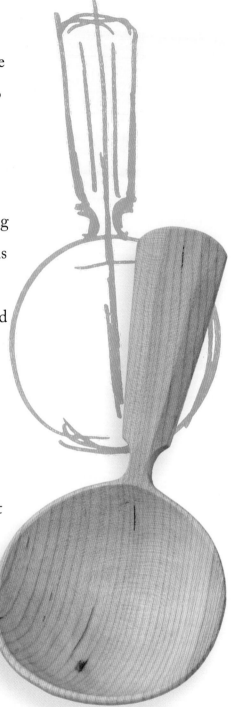

Tools and Materials
- Wood
- Axe
- Club
- Pruning saw
- Sloyd knife
- Hook knife
- Wood finish (optional)

Pattern on page 124

1 **Create the crank face.** Starting with a billet longer than you need, axe in a small crank face. Remember to keep a couple of inches away from the end of the billet, both to protect your fingers and to avoid any cracks in the end grain from drying.

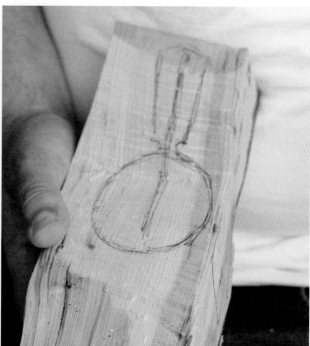

2 **Draw the outline.** I find that round forms are easiest to draw by anchoring the side of my hand on a tabletop and drawing arcs with the pen as I spin the billet around.

3 **Make the usual stop cuts.** Brace the extra billet length against the heel of the axe before cutting.

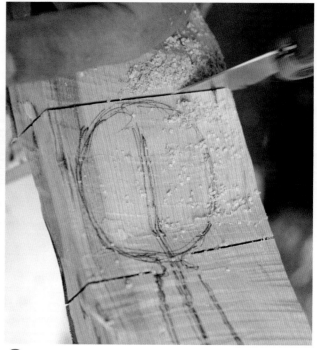

4 **Trim the bowl end.** Then, saw the extra wood from the end of the handle.

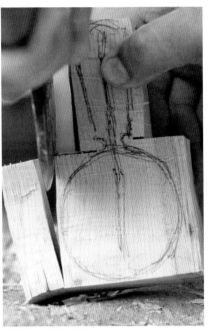

⑤ **Split the handle waste.** Use a series of bump cuts, being cautious not to be so forceful that you carry right through to the bowl and ruin the blank.

⑥ **Split the waste off the side of the bowl.** Use bump cuts. This time, you can be as forceful as you want.

⑦ **Axe around the tip of the bowl.** Stay away from the end grain.

⑧ **Axe the back of the bowl and handle.** First, define the deepest part at the middle, then pull up the sides. Axe around the back shoulders, supporting the neck of the scoop on the edge of the stump.

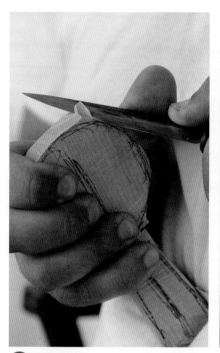
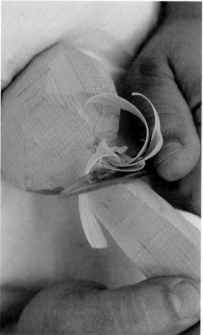

9 **Rough out the outline.** Switching to the sloyd knife, use squeeze cuts to rough out around the bowl. Use pull cuts to rough out the handle, and the tip of the knife and a twisting motion to rough out the neck detail.

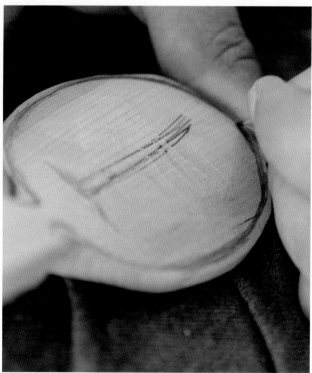

10 **Clean up and refine.** Use rim pivot cuts to clean up the top line of the bowl. Then, clean up the top of the handle by using a pull cut. Finally, use squeeze cuts on the back of the bowl, aiming to refine the rim by removing half its width.

11 **Redraw the form.** Refine the circle of the bowl as well as you can by eye.

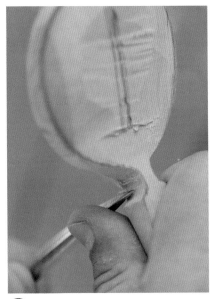

12 **Carve around the outline again.** This time, take care to clean up the neck detail as much as you can.

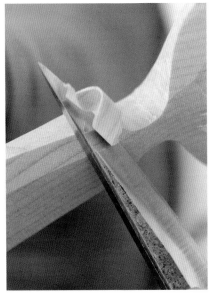

13 **Create facets on the handle.** Using pull cuts, create strong facets down the top of the handle, then soften with microfacets. Facet the back of the handle the same way, then facet the end of the handle.

14 **Rough out the bowl.** Using the hook knife, spin the hole deeper and deeper. When the knife appears to bottom out, clean things up as best you can and stop.

15 **Level the rim with pivot cuts.** Blend the cuts into the neck with squeeze cuts from that direction.

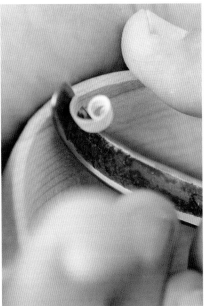

16 **Establish the inner rim with the hook.** Then, clean up the bowl with the usual sequence of cuts. Beware chasing a perfect surface and bottoming out the hook. Microchamfer the inner rim, then the outer rim, being careful to keep the knife from catching in the grain.

17 **Thin the back of the bowl.** Use squeeze cuts, feeling the thickness of the bowl with your thumb and forefinger. When it is as delicate as you dare, burnish and finish the scoop. You're done!

Cooking Spatula

Approximate length: 11" (27.9cm)

This form is a good chance to
practice the cuts needed for a
larger form on something that
is both forgiving (because it is
asymmetrical) and challenging,
because the handle is more
rectangular and therefore more
precise. This is also one of the most
useful spoon designs in this book.

Tools and Materials

- Wood
- Axe
- Club
- Pruning saw
- Sloyd knife
- Hook knife
- Wood finish (optional)

Pattern on page 125

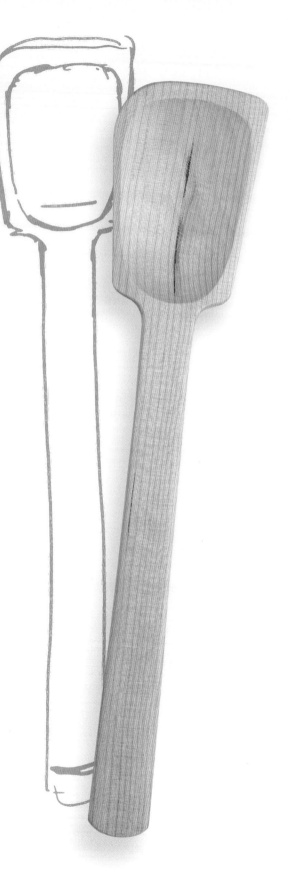

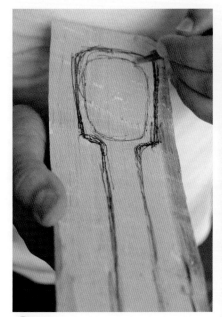

1 **Axe the crank face and draw your outline.** After selecting your wood and shaping your billet, axe in a crank face before drawing the spatula outline.

2 **Trim the billet.** First, trim the bowl end. Make your stop cuts at the neck, then flip it around and trim the handle end. Keep your cuts right up next to the outline. Remember to keep your stop cuts back from the shoulders of the outline.

3 **Split the sides of the bowl.** For this form, you split the sides of the bowl in the reverse direction from what is typical. Because there is a slight taper to the bowl from the tip to the handle, split the waste off with bump cuts, starting at the tip. Then, axe to the line of the sides and around the curve of the bowl tip.

4 **Axe the back of the bowl and handle.** Use relief cuts up the back of the handle before driving the line down. Don't bother axing around the shoulders for this form; it is too easy to remove material you intended to keep.

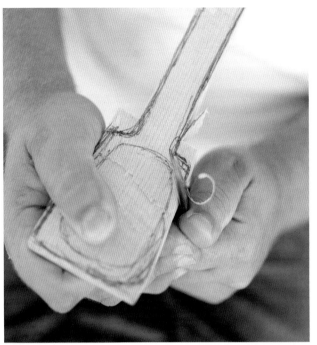

5 **Carve the bowl's outline.** Switching to the sloyd knife, use pull cuts and squeeze cuts to carve to the outline on the bowl. While the bowl outline on most forms is done entirely with squeeze cuts, the straight sides of this shape make pull cuts a good option. Use squeeze cuts to rough out the shoulders of the form, getting underneath any axe or saw marks but not trying to make the surface clean.

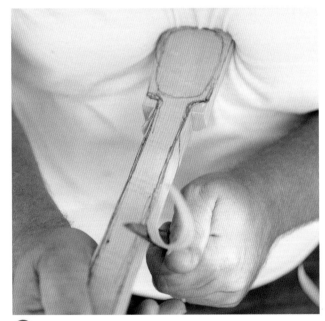

6 **Dress the handle and bowl.** Rough out the handle with pull cuts on the sides and squeeze cuts on the handle end. Dress the top of the form first, using pull cuts for the handle and rim pivot cuts for the top rim. Then, dress the bottom with squeeze cuts for the bowl and pull cuts that shift to knee brace cuts for the handle.

7 **Redraw the outline in pencil.** Be careful to keep the neck nice and wide because it isn't particularly deep.

8 **Carve around the outline.** Start with the front rim of the bowl, using squeeze cuts. Then, use pull cuts for the sides of the bowl and the handle sides. Leave these last cuts attached.

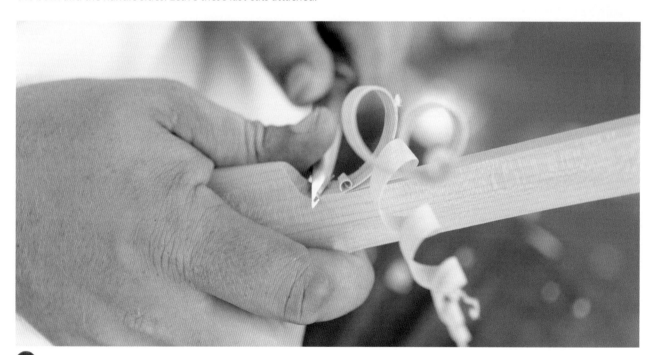

9 **Clean up the neck and shoulders.** Use the tip of the knife and a twisting motion to ease the blade under the handle cuts that have been left attached. Soften the corners of the shoulders and the corner of the bowl tip. Dress the top of the handle one last time, aiming for one bold cut from handle tip to bowl, then dress the back of the spoon with the usual cuts. Again, aim for a single cut defining the back of the handle, giving you a rectangular cross section. On the back of the bowl, define the underside of the rim first, then smooth out the facets with a series of squeeze cuts that end with a pivot of the knife to give you an extra inch or so. Run microchamfers down the handle edges, two per edge so the corner is nicely rounded but still tight. Microchamfer the underside of the rim at the same time, then clean up the handle end.

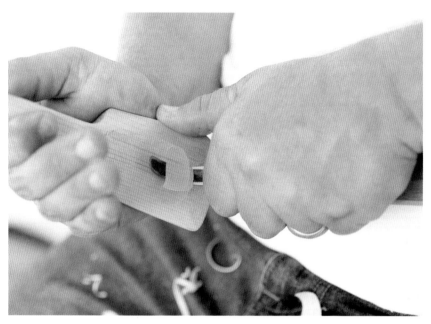

10 **Rough out the bowl with the hook knife.** Start with a series of side-to-side cuts down the center, then switch to cuts that chase around and around in a circle, gradually widening the bowl until you get close to your finished depth and shape.

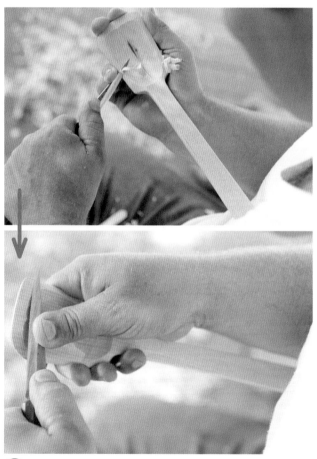

11 **Level the rim.** Use the usual pivot cuts, being careful not to accidentally cut the other rim with the heel of the blade. Microchamfer the outside edge of the rim.

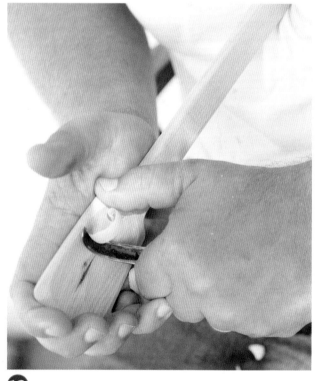

12 **Finish the bowl.** Following the usual sequence, define the inner rim, then refine the curvature of the bowl with a series of cuts going from the tip of the bowl down to the middle. Then, match that in the back shoulders with cuts going from the middle out to the sides. Remember that you can cut with the tip of the hook, pivoting on the heel, or with the heel of the hook, pivoting on the tip. Walk away before you make things worse. Burnish and wax, and it's ready to use!

Ice Cream Scoop

Approximate length: 8¼" (21cm)

This form introduces a new design element: the chunky handle. Such handles can be used in many designs, and they have their own considerations. Ice cream scoops don't function like regular spoons; you plunge an ice cream scoop straight down, and then rely on the curvature of the bowl at the neck to curl the ice cream into a ball so it releases. If you give this form too much crank, it won't work well. Similarly, the bowl needs to be thick at the sides and back for strength, while the rim is thin enough that it cuts into the ice cream.

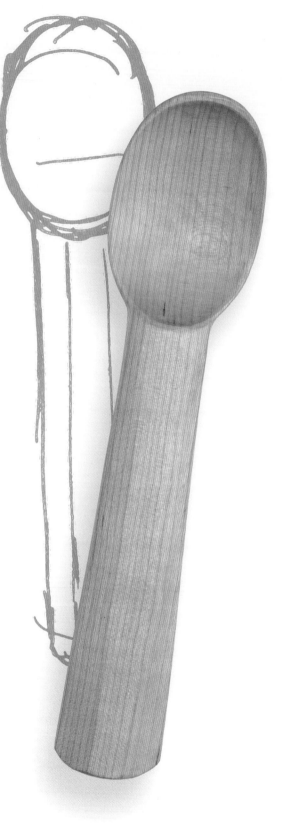

Tools and Materials
- Wood
- Axe
- Club
- Pruning saw
- Sloyd knife
- Hook knife
- Wood finish (optional)

Pattern on page 125

1 **Axe in the crank face.** Start by axing in a crank face that has as little crank as possible. You accomplish this, in part, by not blending the line for the handle with the line for the back of the bowl. Instead of a shallow V shape, you are creating a stretched-out lightning bolt shape, with the zigzag bit going from the handle down to the bottom of the crank.

2 **Draw the outline.** Make sure that the bottom of the crank is lined up with the widest part of the bowl, something you should not do in other forms. Normally, you place the bottom of the crank back on the shoulders to avoid having the grain change at that widest part of the outline, but here you want the two to coincide.

3 **Trim, make stop cuts, and carve the outline.** Trim the bowl end and make your stop cuts, then flip it around and trim the handle end. Switching to the knife, do all the usual cuts to rough out the outline.

4 **Carve the handle facets.** Establish the handle facets on the top and the back using the appropriate cuts. Doing the facets this early helps limit the size of cut you need to dress the top and bottom face, which you should do after you create the facets.

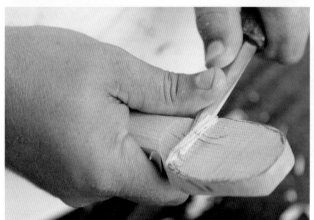

5 **Cut the top rim of the bowl.** Use rim pivot cuts and then squeeze cuts for the back shoulders. If your knife tip isn't sufficiently sharp, you will have trouble cleaning up the lowest part of the rim that corresponds to the change in grain direction. If so, stop and sharpen. Thin down the back of the bowl in the usual manner, making sure to keep it quite thick at the back, even as it tapers to narrow at the rim.

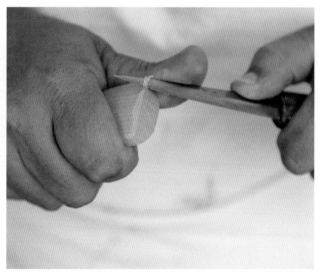

6 **Facet the handle end.** If you like, define the curvature of the edge created between the handle sides and the end by doing squeeze cuts that go across the form, rather than simply from the handle straight up.

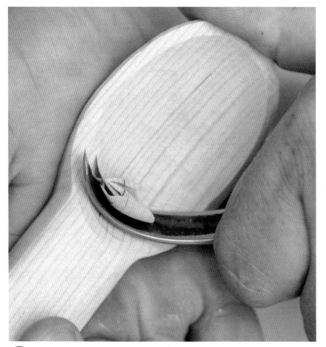

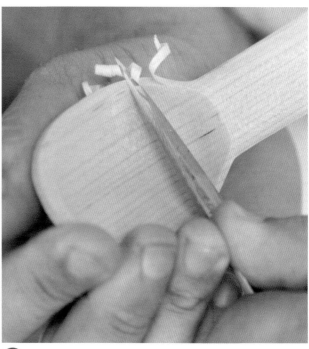

7 **Rough hollow the bowl.** Use all the usual cuts. The bowl should be relatively shallow.

8 **Recut the rim to flatten it.** Take a minute to refine the outline of the bowl where it meets the handle, blending those cuts into the facets.

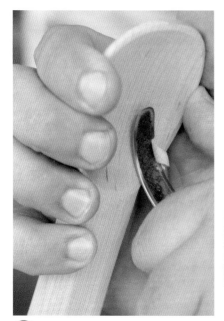

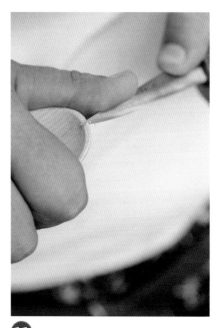

9 **Finish hollowing the bowl.** Use all the usual cuts. Be aware that the grain transition in the bottom of the bowl will be more difficult to negotiate than usual because of how strongly the back shoulders of the bowl are tilted within the grain.

10 **Thin the back of the bowl.** Blend the back shoulders of the bowl into the facets on the back of the handle. Aim to have the rim quite thin at the edge, but then quickly tapered up to a much stronger cross section.

11 **Microchamfer anything that needs it.** This includes all three edges of the rim (inside, outside, and under), as well as the spines between the facets on the handle. Burnish and finish the scoop, then dig in!

Toast Tongs

Approximate length: 9" (22.8cm)

Now we get into some weird techniques. These toast tongs use many of the same cuts and strategies as the previous forms, but the order of operations is necessarily different because they are not a spoon. It is magical, however, to create something that flexes and moves out of an unmoving block of wood. That doesn't get old.

Tools and Materials
- Wood
- Axe
- Club
- Pruning saw
- Drill and drill bit
- Sloyd knife
- Hook knife
- Wood finish (optional)

Pattern on page 125

1 **Axe the face.** Use as clean-grained a piece of wood as you can source. Any sort of squirrely grain will come back to haunt you in this project. You want the grain to be as straight and simple as possible.

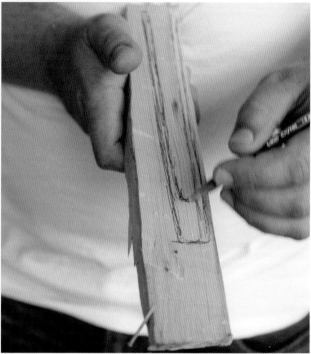

2 **Draw the outline of the tongs, as seen from the side.** That means you are drawing both blades, seen edge-on, and the part at the top that connects them. Each blade should angle just slightly across the grain, and I find it is helpful if the blade tip curves out the tiniest bit.

3 **Trim the billet.** Trim the blade end of the billet with a saw. Do not trim the other end.

5 **Drill holes in the form.** Now for the weird part. Using a drill gun and bit, drill a line of holes down the center of the form between the two blades. If you have a drill press, great; otherwise a drill gun works, but be careful. Use a fresh bit of as large a size that fits in the narrowest part at the top, and hold the billet down against your axing stump. The long handle at the end that you didn't saw off helps keep the billet from simply ripping in two. Start at the blade end and drill a line of holes that just barely touch. Be extra cautious as you approach the handle end.

4 **Axe to the outline you've drawn.** Use all the usual methods.

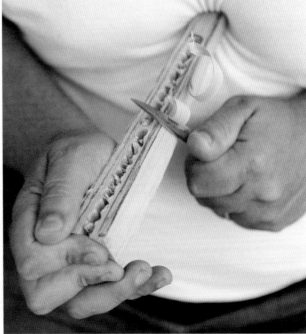

6 **Trim the excess.** With the center successfully drilled out, trim the other end of the billet, taking care not to vibrate the arms too much.

7 **Carve the blades and trim the handle.** Carve the outside of the blades with pull cuts. Trim the handle end with squeeze cuts.

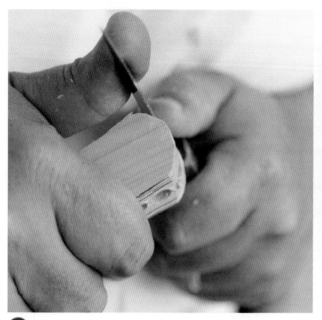

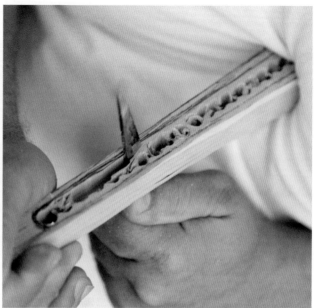

8 **Trim the blades.** Press the blades together and use squeeze cuts to trim both ends at once. Then, cut the edges of both blades at once with pull cuts, going from the blade tips to the junction end. Flip it over and repeat on the other side. Aim to have the same amount of taper on each side.

9 **Rough out the inside of the tongs with pull cuts.** Switch to squeeze cuts to do the bit near the blade ends, slowly working your way down through the waste wood. If you try to do this too quickly, it will exert too strong a twisting force on the wood, so go slow.

10 **Clean up the junction of the two blades.** Use the tip of the knife to clean up the junction of the two blades, twisting it to get under that final drill mark.

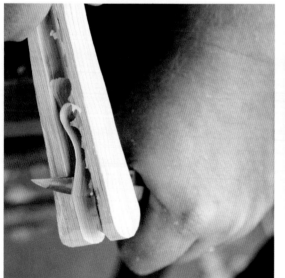

11 **Use squeeze cuts to thin out the insides of the blades further.** Use a knee brace cut to rough out as much material as you can from the inside of the blades. Then switch to squeeze cuts to further refine them. Give each blade some camber, meaning thicker in the center and thinner towards the edges, if you cut a cross section out of the wood. The easiest way to do this is to define the edges of the blades first, on both the inside and the outside.

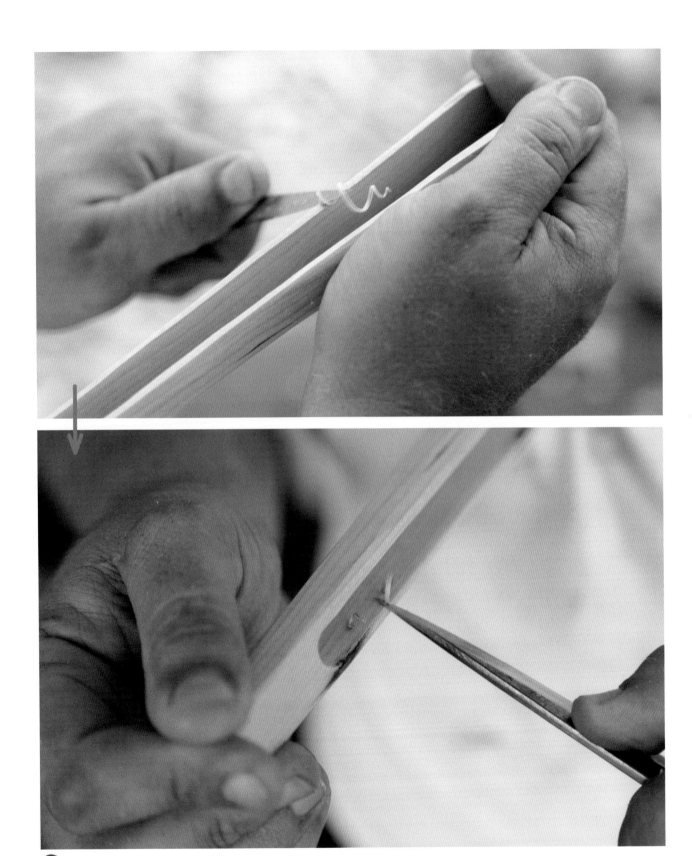

12 **Chamfer all relevant edges.** Soften the corners, but don't use strong cuts. Burnish and finish, and they are ready to use!

Flour Scoop

Approximate length 9" (22.8cm)

It makes sense that this flour scoop would be one of the final endeavors in a book like this—one that tries to stack projects so that you are continually challenged as you progress through them. The sheer size of the thing requires more force to pull off, while the amount of material in the bowl to be removed is a marathon and presents some fancy footwork at the end. In addition, the open front of the form means that it is relatively weak and susceptible to crushing forces applied while carving. Take care not to destroy this with your own awesome strength as you carve it.

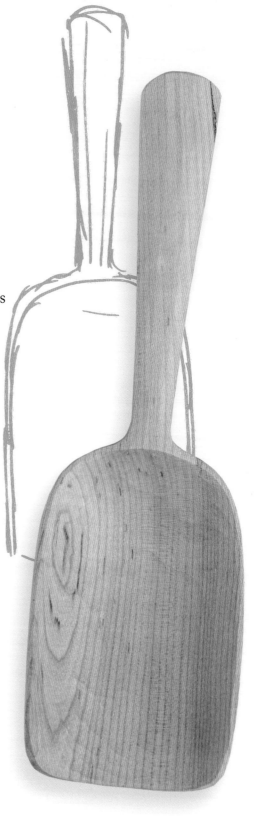

Tools and Materials
- Wood
- Axe
- Club
- Pruning saw
- Sloyd knife
- Hook knife
- Wood finish (optional)

Pattern on page 123

1 **Axe in a shallow crank face.** Have as much wood on the bowl end as on the handle end. It is easy to start with too thick of a billet. Two or three inches is fine.

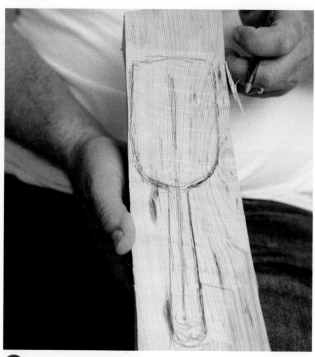

2 **Draw the outline.** Make sure to orient the shoulders of the form on the bottom of the crank.

3 **Trim the end of the billet.** Be sure to make the usual stop cuts at the neck.

4 **Remove waste from the handle sides.** Use bump down cuts followed by pop cuts. Axe the sides of the bowl to the outline.

5 **Add bevels to the bowl.** Bevel the back of the bowl with some strong facets, made with the axe.

6 **Axe a curve into the end of the bowl.** Do this gently. Just a little bit will do.

7 **Bevel the back shoulders of the bowl.** Support the neck of the scoop on the edge of the stump and axe around the outline of the shoulders. Bevel the back shoulders of the bowl, tapering the facet off as you reach the handle. Axe down the back of the handle.

8 **Rough out the outline.** Use pull cuts on the bowl sides and handle and squeeze cuts on the bowl end, shoulders, and handle end.

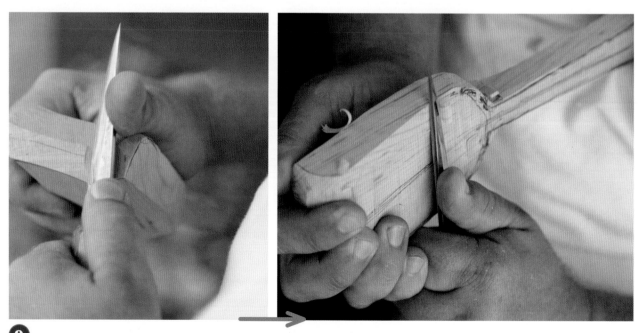

9 **Refine the rim.** Use squeeze cuts to refine the curve of the front rim of the scoop, blending between the sides and the front edge. Use pivot cuts to finish refining the rim and blend them into the neck.

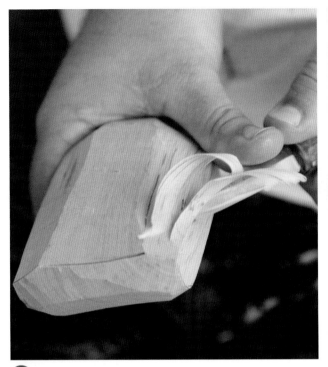

10 **Rough out the form.** Rough out the back of the bowl with squeeze cuts. Dress the top of the handle with pull cuts and the back of the handle with knee brace cuts.

11 **Redraw the shape.** Using a pencil, redraw the flour scoop's shape.

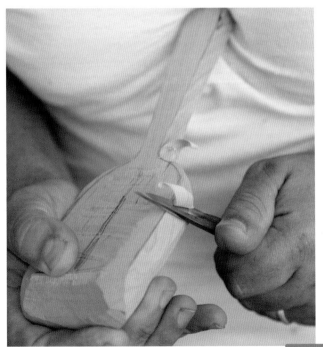

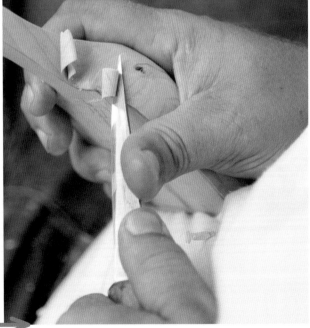

12 **Recut the outline.** Use all the usual cuts, paying particular attention to cleaning up the shoulders, which tend to be too fat, as they are difficult to cut across so much end grain.

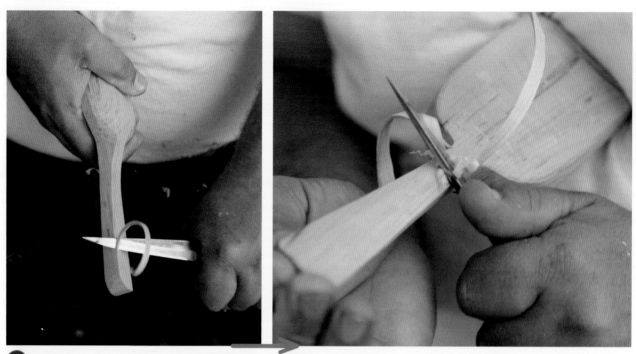

13 **Chamfer and facet the handle.** Chamfer the top and bottom of the handle, and facet the handle end. Apply microchamfers as needed.

14 **Start hollowing the bowl.** This will take a long time, so pace yourself. Start with mostly side-to-side cuts, and nibble at the wood rather than trying to take off big pieces. Be careful not to let the wood chip off the end grain when cutting the front of the bowl, and don't let your cuts go too deep here.

15 **Continue hollowing.** As you get to the middle of the hollowing process, alternate between cutting from the rim down to the middle and from the middle up to the rim. Don't neglect the back shoulders!

16 **Finish hollowing the scoop.** Use a series of smoothing cuts from the tip of the bowl down towards the shoulders. You won't be able to do these straight back, but will need to have them angling across the grain somewhat so that the knife doesn't dig in. Microchamfer the inner rim with the hook knife.

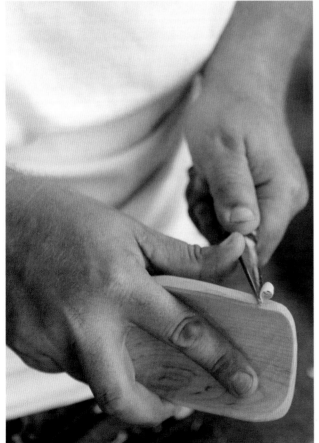

17 **Thin the back of the bowl and blend it into the handle.** Once you have cleaned up the bowl as much as possible, thin the back of the bowl to achieve the right level of delicacy. In general, it will feel thick and clunky until, suddenly, it doesn't. Make sure to work your way to this level of delicacy all over so you can reduce the amount of force you are applying to the form, both through your knife and from your hands squeezing the wood, as you approach the final thickness. Pay particular attention to thinning the back of the shoulders, blending them into the handle. When you're happy with everything, add microchamfers to the outer rim (on this form there is no under rim), burnish, and finish!

Everyday Spoon

Approximate length 8" (20.3cm)

Please note: if you have skipped all the way to this form without reading through the others, you will be missing all the cumulative explanations I have given along the way in the step-by-step instructions. There is a reason this form is last. It is one of the most difficult forms to do well, interacting as it does with food, dishes, and your mouth. In many ways, it is the culmination of everything I have articulated throughout this book. While I have provided more step-by-step pictures, I have not exhaustively written out the process as though you are coming to this without the benefit of everything that has come before. So be warned.

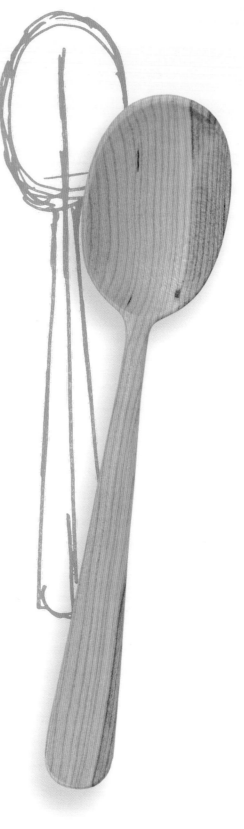

Tools and Materials
- Wood
- Axe
- Club
- Pruning saw
- Sloyd knife
- Hook knife
- Wood finish (optional)

Pattern on page 122

1 **Begin axing in the crank face.** Maintain several inches distance from the end of the billet. This is both to keep your fingers safe and to eliminate the risk of any air-drying cracks from being in the wood.

2 **Axe in the handle end of the crank face.** Raise and lower the handle end of the billet to make a top surface that has the top line of the spoon you want in it. I prefer my handles to have a tail flip and a bit of dolphin back as they approach the bowl.

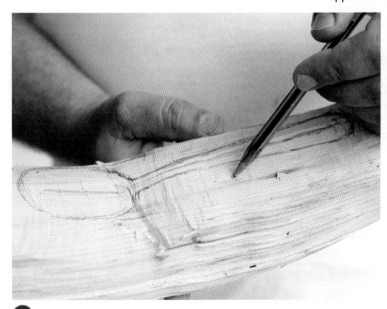

3 **Draw your outline in pen and trim.** Start with the bowl, then the centerline, then the handle. Trim the bowl end, then saw in the stop cuts, then trim the handle end.

4 **Reduce the bowl thickness and remove waste.** Axe the back of the bowl and the back of the handle to reduce its thickness. Remove waste from the handle with bump cuts and pop cuts.

 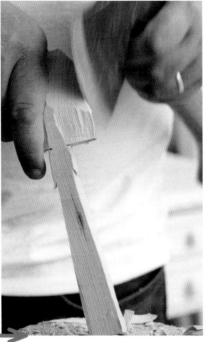 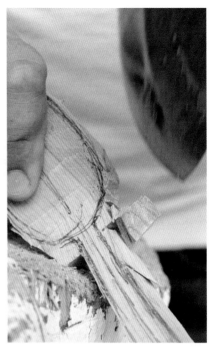

⑤ **Axe around the bowl and back shoulders.** Tilt the blank progressively further to follow the curve. Remember, the blank moves, but the axe stays in the same position, moving straight up and down. Axe the sides of the back of the bowl, drawing the rim up. Flip the blank around and axe in the back shoulders of the spoon.

⑥ **Axe around the shoulder of the bowl.** Support the neck on the edge of the stump. Axe down the back of the handle. Switching to the sloyd knife, carve around the bowl, then the sides of the handle.

 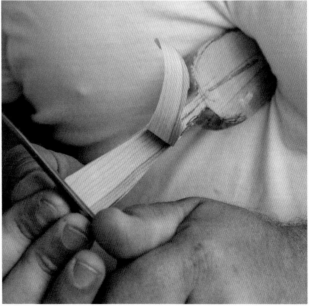

⑦ **Rough out the neck outline.** Use twisting squeeze cuts in the neck of the spoon to get underneath any axe or saw marks.

⑧ **Rough out the top of the handle.** Use a series of pull cuts, creating the profile that you want. Switch to a squeeze cut right at the neck so you have more control over how the cuts interact with the back rim of the bowl.

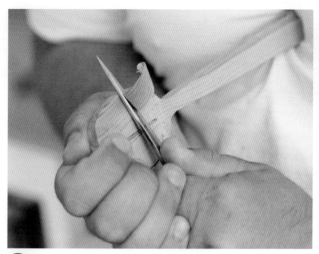

9 **Cut the line of the top rim using rim pivot cuts.** Remember that the force is always exerted in the opposite direction of the pivot, keeping your hand and body safe.

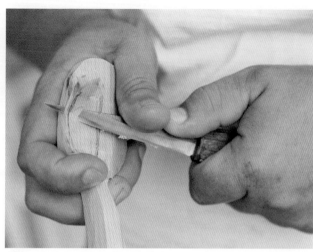

10 **Cut the other side of the bowl using the second rim pivot cut.** At the start of the cut, cheat your thumb over to the side a fraction of an inch so you can get your knife tip in there.

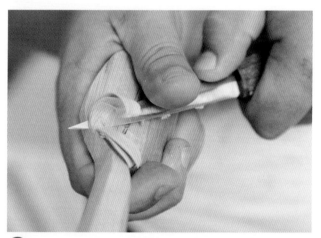

11 **Finish the second pivot cut.** Shift your finger placement to get it out of the way once you no longer need it to stabilize the spoon.

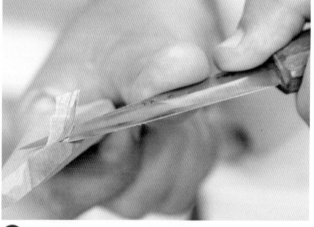

12 **Pull up the rim on the back of the bowl.** Use squeeze cuts, first defining the centerline, then blending out to the sides.

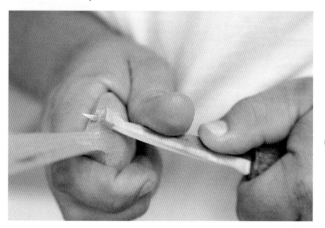

13 **Reduce the back shoulders.** Use squeeze cuts to reduce the back shoulders of the bowl, twisting the tip of the knife as you approach the neck to avoid overcutting. Reduce the back of the handle with pull cuts that shift seamlessly into chest brace cuts.

14 **Redraw the outline with a sharp pencil.** Define the neck first, then draw the bowl, then mark the end of the handle that will line up with the bowl. Finally, draw the sides of the handle.

15 **Recut to the new line.** Start with the sides of the handle. Leave these cuts attached and go on to cut around the bowl outline.

16 **Clean up the neck.** Use twisting squeeze cuts, coming around the shoulder and easing under the cuts that were left attached at the neck.

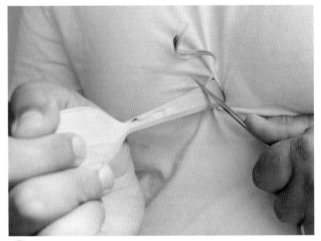

17 **Pull chamfers down the back of the handle.** Go from the bowl to the handle end. Use pull cuts that shift to chest brace cuts. Then, chamfer the edges of this main chamfer.

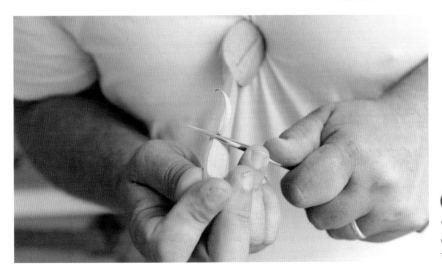

18 **Chamfer the top of the handle with pull cuts.** Take care to ease them out as you approach the neck. Chamfer the edges of this new chamfer.

19 Chamfer the handle end. Cut sideways to the handle to follow the outline.

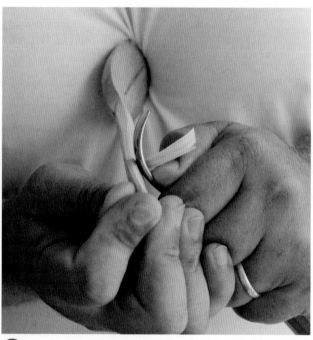

20 Hollow the tail flip. Switching to the hook knife, use it in a pull cut like you would a sloyd knife to hollow the tail flip just slightly. Blend this into the rest of the handle.

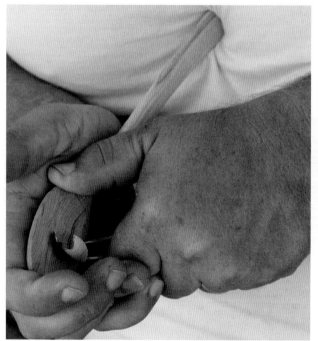

21 Rough out the bowl with the hook knife. Choke up on the blade and brace your thumb so you have something to pull toward. Exit cuts by swirling to the side, either moving the blade or moving the spoon against the blade. Continue until you are close to your finished depth and rim thickness.

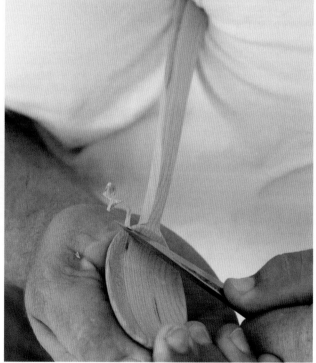

22 Level the rim. Switching to the sloyd, level the rim using the usual two pivot cuts. Be careful not to cut the opposite side with the heel of the blade.

23 **Define the rim and smooth the bowl.** Define the inner rim with the hook knife, then build a series of smoothing cuts from the tip of the bowl down into the bottom of the crank.

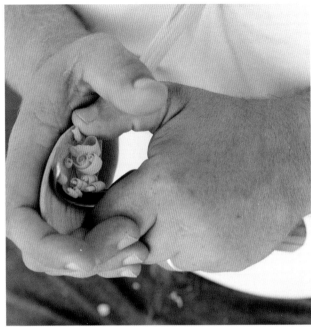

24 **Finish smoothing the bowl.** Cut from the center up to the edges, being careful to keep the knife cutting and not digging into the grain.

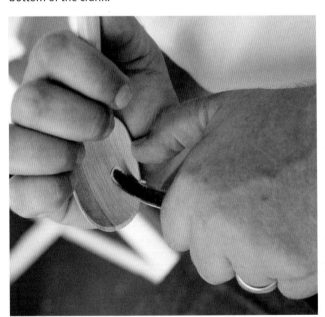

25 **Microchamfer the inner rim.** Use a hook knife and keep the rim as tiny as you can.

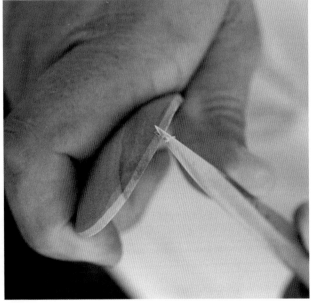

26 **Microchamfer the outer rim.** Use the sloyd knife. Take care to keep the knife perpendicular to the plane of the spoon to avoid splitting the wood.

27 **Thin the back of the bowl with a series of squeeze cuts.** Keep at it until the spoon has the right feel in your mouth or to your fingers. Aim to keep it thickest in the center and tapering toward the edges. Flip the spoon around and thin the back shoulders the same way, taking care to avoid splitting the wood where the grain changes. Microchamfer the underside of the rim. Burnish and finish the spoon. Enjoy!

Patterns
Photocopy all patterns at 125%

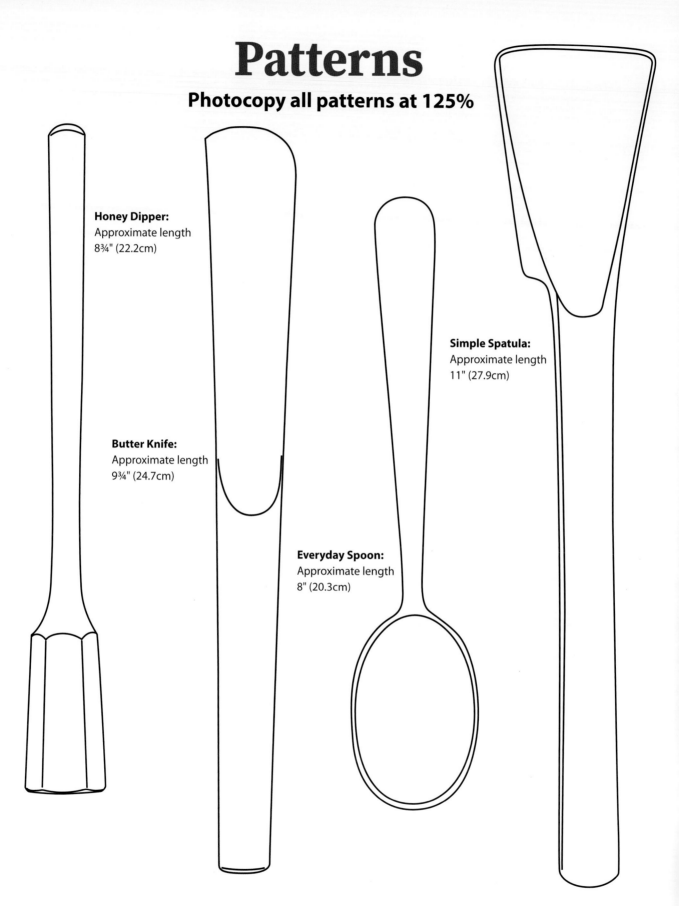

Honey Dipper:
Approximate length
8¾" (22.2cm)

Butter Knife:
Approximate length
9¾" (24.7cm)

Everyday Spoon:
Approximate length
8" (20.3cm)

Simple Spatula:
Approximate length
11" (27.9cm)

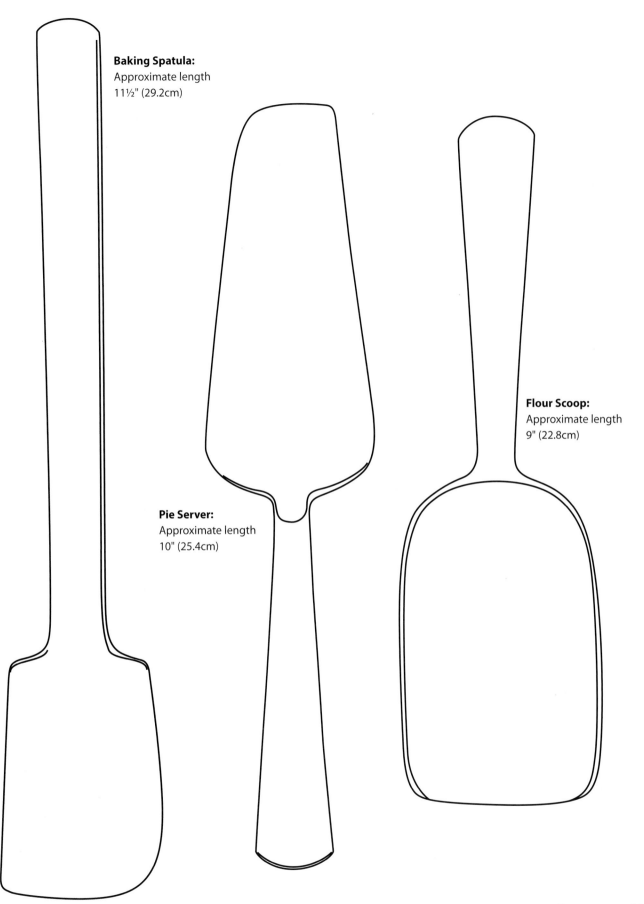

Baking Spatula:
Approximate length
11½" (29.2cm)

Pie Server:
Approximate length
10" (25.4cm)

Flour Scoop:
Approximate length
9" (22.8cm)

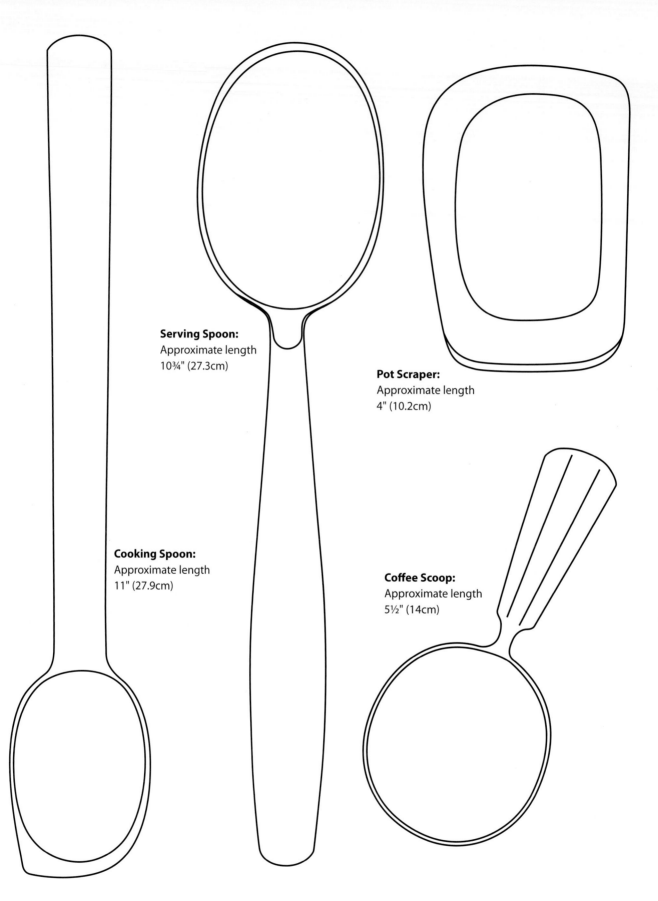

Serving Spoon:
Approximate length
10¾" (27.3cm)

Pot Scraper:
Approximate length
4" (10.2cm)

Cooking Spoon:
Approximate length
11" (27.9cm)

Coffee Scoop:
Approximate length
5½" (14cm)

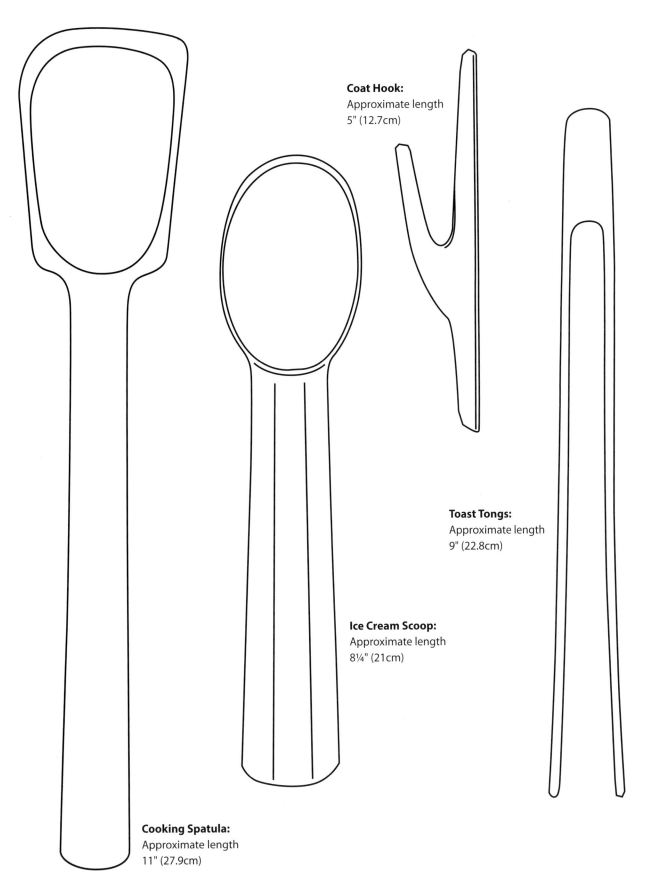

Coat Hook:
Approximate length
5" (12.7cm)

Toast Tongs:
Approximate length
9" (22.8cm)

Ice Cream Scoop:
Approximate length
8¼" (21cm)

Cooking Spatula:
Approximate length
11" (27.9cm)

Index

Note: Page numbers in *italics* indicate projects and patterns *(in parentheses)*.

About the Author

Emmet Van Driesche is a full-time professional spoon carver and the publisher of *Spoonesaurus Magazine*, a print-only quarterly dedicated to the craft and culture of spoon carving. He is the author of three previous books: *The Land Before Us*, a book of poems about his time working as a tall ships sailor, *Carving Out a Living on the Land*, a memoir of taking over a 60-year-old Christmas tree farm, and *Greenwood Spoon Carving*, the in-depth companion to this book you are holding. The best place to go to learn more about these books and his work is *www.emmetvandriesche.com*. You can find Emmet on Instagram @emmet_van_driesche or listen to his daily short-form podcast, Emmet Audio, wherever you get your podcasts.

About the Photographer

Ben Gancsos is a commercial photographer, documenting architecture, interiors, and people. A thousand spoons after stumbling upon the wacky world of greenwood carving, he co-founded NYC Spoon Club, a monthly gathering of likeminded urban carvers, in 2018. He now calls the most forested of the states home and, still true to his urban spoon carver roots, he resides in the city of Portland, Maine with his wife and daughter. His website is www.gancsos.com and his spoons can be seen on Instagram @bgancsos.